Teaching information skills
Theory and practice

Teaching information skills
Theory and practice

Jo Webb and Chris Powis

facet publishing

Published by
Facet Publishing
7 Ridgmount Street
London WC1E 7AE

Facet Publishing is wholly owned by CILIP: the Chartered Institute of
Library and Information Professionals.

First published 2004

British Library Cataloguing in Publication Data
A catalogue record for this book is available from the British Library.

ISBN 1-85604-513-7

Typeset in 11/15 pt Bergamo and Chantilly by Stephen York.
Printed and made in Great Britain by MPG Books Ltd, Bodmin,
Cornwall.

Contents

Foreword

As both a former academic librarian who spent many hours trying to teach information skills to students and a Library and Information Science educator, I welcome this timely book. In every sector of the knowledge economy, information professionals are being asked to support lifelong learning by enabling members of their community to equip themselves with the skills they need to make effective and relevant use of information: effective use of information for personal and social life, for learning, for work, for political empowerment and for creativity and enjoyment. Information literacy is one of the key skills we all need; too often the concentration is on the technology and not on the content or effective use of the information provided.

This book, written by experienced practitioners, provides a good introduction to the theory underpinning the teaching or facilitation of information skills as well as practical tips and case studies. All too often the theory is ignored, but for all information professionals seeking to design and implement information skills programmes it is crucial that we understand how people learn. The focus in the book is clearly on the needs of learners. It encourages information professionals to step back from the pragmatics of delivering information skills teaching to reflect on the 'why' and 'how' and to facilitating learning in a wide range of contexts. The advice and guidance offered to information professionals working in different sectors is both thoughtful and practical.

The importance of teamworking and collaboration which the book endorses is also welcome. Working across sectors and across different domains can only serve to strengthen the drive to information literacy. Shared experience and expertise of teaching information skills and supporting learning should enhance and improve professional practice. Staff working in all sectors should find this book helpful whether they have been teaching information skills for some time or are just beginning to offer sessions to support learning at any level.

Margaret Watson
President
Chartered Institute of Library and Information Professionals
2003–4

Acknowledgements

We would like to thank the colleagues and teachers who have helped us to develop our own theory and practice in teaching. Special mention must be made of those colleagues who helped us with the case studies, and especially Isla Kuhn from the Clinical Sciences Library at the University of Leicester, Nigel Morgan and Linda Davies of Cardiff University and Jane Mortimer at De Montfort University, whose stories you will read.

Jo would like to thank Robert Richardson and Claire Mactavish in the Faculty of Humanities, De Montfort University, from whom she learnt about informal and collaborative teaching. There are numerous colleagues in library and information services and in the world of higher education who have been role models and guides, including Jane Clarke and Sally Brown. Special acknowledgement is due to those whom she has persuaded to speak at UC&R events through the years on learning and teaching issues (Tracy, David, Ruth, Jo, Sue and so many more). Lastly, she would like to thank library staff at De Montfort University for their good humour and support while she bored them talking about what she was writing next.

Chris thanks Cathy Carpmael and Jan Nicholls, who were his first teaching mentors, and his colleagues at Nene College (later University College Northampton), especially Jane Marshall, Alan Rosling and Heather McBryde-Wilding. The EduLib Development Officers, especially Sheila Padden and David Pennie, and the project team, in particular David McNamara, Jane Core and Victoria Eaton, were great influences on his teaching development. Chris cites as his inspirations his family, closely followed by Derek Dougan, John Richards, Steve Bull, John Ford, Flann O'Brien, Van Morrison and Laurel and Hardy.

Finally, our gratitude to Margaret Oldroyd, who set us on the way to getting published, and Margaret Watson for her enthusiastic response to our ideas.

1 Introduction

This book is not about whether librarians should be teachers or the importance of information literacy. Other people have written, and are currently writing, on these themes far more fluently and coherently than we ever could. Instead we have produced a text about how to teach and support learning in our very specific occupational context. The way we decided to do this was by combining theory, practice and case studies mainly imaginary in their details but true in their fundamentals. In each chapter you will find a discussion of the topic, which reviews the points and principles of the main theory, some practical hints and tips and usually two case studies that discuss a real-life learning and teaching challenge encountered by an information professional.

Background

When we were researching the book we were surprised to find that there were very few titles that tried to do what we wanted to. Books about how to teach and support learning tend either to be very practical (like Race, 1999), very specific (Brown and Knight, 1994) or theoretical (Light and Cox, 2001). And of course most of the texts are written for professional teachers or academics. Only Milne and Noone (1996) and Peterson (1992) were written for non-teachers and they do not cover all we felt it would be helpful to say about teaching and supporting learning as a library and information professional.

At the same time our experience of running courses, attending conferences and meeting colleagues made us very aware that there is a genuine demand for personal and professional development across the community within the UK and more widely. Projects like EduLib, which ran a series of courses across the UK in the mid-1990s, and the level of interest in the Big Blue project (www.leeds.ac.uk/bigblue/) only confirmed our opinions. However, not everyone can or will attend a course on how to teach. You may not be able to because of resource limitations in terms of time or money, or because you have no accessible training and development opportunities. We hope that, if this is the case, this work will get you started on the way to becoming an effective teacher. Alternatively, you may just want to explore a specific theme, to reflect on delivery methods or assessment techniques for example. Here again we hope this book will help by condensing and presenting theory in an accessible way to the practitioner.

Our decision to write this book was based on some strongly held beliefs. The first was that in order to be effective at teaching and supporting learning you need to adopt a reflective and professional approach, defined in the first instance by understanding something of the principles and processes involved in good learning and teaching. Secondly, we wanted to illustrate the tremendous range and variety of what could be defined as information skills teaching. Thirdly, we wanted to give you the confidence to experiment and discover your own voice or style as teachers and learning facilitators.

We have tried to avoid relying too much on the largely insular library and information studies literature in our review of theory, and instead have related our work to the more general literature of teaching and learner support. We believe that if you want to be good at teaching and supporting learners you need to have a knowledge of this literature and follow best practice. At the same time, we recognize that our circumstances and opportunities are different from people more regularly employed as teachers and trainers. This is most noticeable in the limited control we have in determining the nature of our encounter with learners and often in our relative lack of power within the teaching or tutoring relationship. Although some people object to being seen as a support service (discussed in Julien and Given, 2003), our occupational role in supporting learning is most often to facilitate, assist, guide and develop. This is still real teaching and learning support, even if we sometimes feel that our work lacks status and recognition.

You will find the influence of the EduLib project (McNamara and Core, 1998) running throughout this text. This is not too surprising because one of the authors was an EduLib development officer, and the experience coloured much of his professional practice. More profoundly, in our view EduLib was a genuinely commendable project, since it enabled British academic librarians to take a course that was built around input from some of the very best and most influential teachers and writers on teaching in higher education. EduLib provided a model syllabus for learning and teaching development that has been cascaded within and outside the UK. However, EduLib did not discuss theory in as much detail as we do, nor did it integrate learning technology within the text as a whole. The work by McNamara and Core (1998) is very much a 'how to guide' for running a course on teaching skills for librarians, not a summary of research and thinking to aid you directly in planning and delivery.

Critics of this book might observe that we have not strayed very far away from our work in higher education libraries, since many of the writers we refer to write specifically about university teaching. We recognize that this is a fair comment, but in our defence our experience as practitioners, trainers and authors shows us that these principles and approaches are valid in our wider professional context. Much of the writing about university teaching is based on encouraging students to become effective and independent learners. Whatever our organizational contexts, be they in public or workplace libraries or educational institutions, library and information professionals also aspire to create a knowledge and information-empowered community of users. Thus we have shared goals, and a common understanding of the voluntary nature of much of the learning activities with which we are involved. We hope, however, that the variety and range of case studies in different occupational sectors will not only compensate for some of this perceived bias in the theory, but demonstrate the wider application of those principles and ideas, thus confirming our point.

Some definitions

Definitions of terms that we use throughout the book are given below.

Teaching

This is the process of when a teacher (see below) shapes a learning experience for an individual or a group. Teaching may take place face-to-face, in a classroom or online, and in a wide variety of formal and informal locations.

Learning

The definition we cite in the next chapter comes from Barker (1998, 7): learning is a 'permanent or temporary change in behaviour or knowledge that arises in consequence of internal or external stimulus'. There is a much wider definition from the Museums, Libraries and Archives Council (a UK Government body):

> Learning is the process of active engagement with experience. It is what people do when they want to make sense of the world. It may involve the development or deepening of skills, knowledge, understanding, awareness, values, ideas and feelings, or an increase in the capacity to reflect. Effective learning leads to change, development and the desire to learn more.
>
> (MLA, 2004)

Learning is not what happens within formal education systems or on organized training courses; it is part of the fundamental human experience. Because libraries are gateways to knowledge, by their very existence they facilitate learning. Library and information professionals may have a hidden role in supporting learning, creating and maintaining systems and services that stimulate learning and are accessible to all. Often, however, we mediate in the learning experience through direct, structured contact with learners. This is what we define as teaching.

Teacher

This is someone who organizes learning and helps the learner to construct meaning. Often the role of the teacher is to shape the learning experience and guide the learner to reach specific goals. The teacher is in control of the narrative process that underpins much teaching. By this we mean that the teacher shapes a story, an experience for the learner. There is usually a beginning, when aims, objectives and learning outcomes are set and the ideas presented; a middle, where ideas are developed and the learner tests out the new knowledge or skills with the teacher; and an end, where the learner is assessed. Teachers are important: very few of us learn without someone to help us make sense of it all. Our use of the term teacher does not necessarily imply someone working exclusively in an educational institution, just someone who teaches formally, or informally. Sometimes we will use the term tutor. We make no distinctions between those two terms.

Student or learner

This is the person who is the object of our teaching activities. We have tried to use the term student when we are writing specifically about learners in educational institutions and learners at any other time. But in our minds the terms are interchangeable: the purpose of being a student is to learn – at least within the pages of this book.

Learning and teaching event

By this we mean a discrete experience built around specific aims, objectives and learning outcomes. The event may be a single session in a classroom, a course or informal tutoring. It may happen face-to-face or online. E-learning is still learning, and to do it well requires the same understanding of pedagogy as in conventional teaching and learner support. Within the learning and teaching event you will usually find someone in the role of teacher or facilitator, and someone in that of learner or group of learners.

Information literacy

As we stated in our first paragraph, this book is not about information literacy, but we do need to consider how information literacy as a normative or external requirement will shape the content of your teaching. As subject specialist librarians, our personal contribution to most formal educational programmes has been through providing contextualized information and academic skills input. When we have run assessed models we have tended to identify from our own understanding of the subject the content and nature of what we wished to teach, using our own conceptualization of subjects and local guidelines rather than library and information-defined standards. For us the means of achieving information literacy is through working within the subject benchmarks and the academic discourse of the subject, rather than rigidly adhering to external definitions of information literacy. On the other hand, we recognize that despite customization many of the learning outcomes in information skills are generic – drawing up keywords, planning a search strategy and so on. Information literacy standards can be helpful benchmarks when designing and developing your content.

The information literacy agenda is both popular and powerful, although the meaning of information literacy itself can be rather difficult to pin down.

The skills agenda

The development of appropriate and effective learning and study skills within education and to support lifelong learning and development has been part of British educational strategy for more than ten years. This is made manifest in a number of ways, ranging from the definition of key skills in post-16 learning to the adoption of 'learning to learn' modules within British universities (Cottrell, 2001). Study and academic skills are formally recognized within the university curriculum (Great Britain, QAA, 2004) and are important in both vocational training and workforce development.

Commonly the range of skills defined within formal education includes the application of number, problem solving and communication skills. Information literacy or information skills are not explicitly mentioned, but are implicit within the communication and IT skills sets. In many educational institutions in the UK the study skills agenda has created opportunities for library and information professional input into formal programmes through standalone modules or integrated into the curriculum. There are varying levels of customization, with some programmes covering the skills in very abstract ways: 'An introduction to report-writing', or contextualized in the discipline: 'To write an essay in English you need to . . .'.

In *Information Capability*, Corrall (2003) describes the information professional's role migration from 'information provision to skills development' through 'a spectrum of interventions' (Corrall, 2003, 2). It is noteworthy that this role is not restricted to the academic library and information service since effective learning skills are required to support lifelong learning and the changing requirements of work and society. Thus we return from a definition of skills and competences to the learner-centred approach that we are advocating throughout this book.

The Big Six Skills

According to the devisers Eisenberg and Berkowitz (1990, 1), the Big Six Skills are a 'general problem-solving approach to library and information instruction'. The skills are process-based and follow a logical order:

- task definition
- information-seeking strategies
- location and access
- use of information
- synthesis
- evaluation.

The Big Six Skills taxonomy is mainly targeted at people working in schools, although it can be applied at other levels. The approach is very similar to the one advocated in much traditional library user education: thinking through the information search process before actually conducting the search. Although Johnston and Webber (2003, 338) comment that it is rather too much like a 'recipe' for success, we think the Big Six Skills have much to recommend them at least in helping you to think through the processes and practicalities of library-based instruction.

Frameworks of information literacy

Johnston and Webber (2003) discuss three of the most important frameworks or models of information literacy.

The ALA model

The current model most often cited comes from the American Library Association: 'Information Literacy is the set of skills needed to find, retrieve, analyze, and use information' (ALA, 2003).

The Seven Pillars of Wisdom

The second model is from the UK and was produced by the Society of College, National and University Libraries' Task Force on Information Skills (now called the Advisory Committee on Information Literacy). This was a more relativist model called the 'Seven Pillars of Wisdom' (SCONUL, 1999).

The seven headline skills are:

1. The ability to recognize a need for information.
2. The ability to distinguish ways in which the information 'gap' may be addressed:
    • knowledge of appropriate kinds of resources, both print and non-print
    • selection of resources with 'best fit' for task at hand
    • the ability to understand the issues affecting accessibility of sources.
3. The ability to construct strategies for locating information:
    • to articulate information need to match against resources

- to develop a systematic method appropriate for the need
- to understand the principles of construction and generation of databases.

4. The ability to locate and access information:
   - to develop appropriate searching techniques (e.g. use of Boolean)
   - to use communication and information technologies, including terms international academic networks
   - to use appropriate indexing and abstracting services, citation indexes and databases
   - to use current awareness methods to keep up to date.

5. The ability to compare and evaluate information obtained from different sources:
   - awareness of bias and authority issues
   - awareness of the peer review process of scholarly publishing
   - appropriate extraction of information matching the information need.

6. The ability to organize, apply and communicate information to others in ways appropriate:
   - to the situation
   - to cite bibliographic references in project reports and theses
   - to construct a personal bibliographic system
   - to apply information to the problem at hand
   - to communicate effectively using appropriate medium
   - to understand issues of copyright and plagiarism.

7. The ability to synthesise and build upon existing information, contributing to the creation of new knowledge.

  (www.sconul.ac.uk/activities/inf-lit/papers/Seven-pillars.html)

In each area the learner would move through levels of competence from novice to expert: 'First year undergraduates will largely be at the bottom of the [model], perhaps only practising the first four skills, whilst postgraduate and research students will aim to be towards the expert end, and will be aspiring to the seventh' (SCONUL, 1999, 8).

This was a helpful approach in as much as there was an attempt to map the development of information skills onto different levels of learning outcomes at university level. We must confess that we have not been entirely convinced by some of the attempts to elaborate the model further (Godwin, 2003). After all, it is common sense and standard pedagogical practice that we should prepare outcomes linked to particular levels of study. So the learning outcomes for a session on historical research methods would be different when working with school pupils or family historians from if we were working with Masters students, even if we might touch on some of the same topics.

A relational model

The third approach is from Australia, where information literacy has had a much higher profile since the early 1990s. Information literacy is not only recognized more widely within the curriculum but is also seen as a key to social inclusion (Johnston and Webber, 2003, 339). Perhaps the most influential writer currently on information literacy comes from Australia. In her important text, *The Seven Faces of Information Literacy* (1997) Christine Bruce used a phenomenographic approach to propose a relational model of information literacy, quite different from the behavioural approaches previously described. According to Bruce information literacy is experienced in varying ways depending on how the information user (the subject) relates to information (the object). The various conceptions are:

- Information literacy is seen as using information technology for information retrieval and communication (The information technology conception)
- Information literacy is seen as finding information (The information sources conception)
- Information literacy is seen as executing a process (The information conception)
- Information literacy is seen as controlling information (The information control conception)
- Information literacy is seen as building up a personal knowledge base in a new area of interest (The knowledge construction conception)

- Information literacy is seen as working with knowledge and personal perspectives adopted in such a way that novel insights are gained. (The knowledge extension conception)
- Information literacy is seen as using information wisely for the benefit of others (The wisdom conception)

(Bruce, 1997, 154)

Following Bruce's argument, we move from objective definitions of knowledge and information to a subjective one, and through to transformational definitions. Bruce argues that information literacy should move away from a description of attributes. Instead an information literacy curriculum must emphasize conceptions and experience. Students therefore will 'learn skills and knowledge within a broader framework of learning to conceive the effective use of information in different ways' (Bruce, 1997, 169).

So information literacy is about information in an abstract sense and how it may be conceived in different ways depending on circumstance. It encompasses computer literacy, library skills, information skills and study skills. Should you wish to review the content of information literacy programmes and more discussion of the standards, we refer you to The Information Literacy Place (http://dis.shef.ac.uk/literacy/default.htm), which has all the necessary links and is an excellent starting point.

Digital literacy and multiliteracies

There is another growing literature (Bawden, 2001) exploring other notions of literacy, including library literacy, computer and IT literacy, media literacy and digital literacy. Omitted by Bawden but of increasing interest is visual literacy (Andretta, 2004). From the discipline of language and linguistics education comes the idea of multiliteracies, a broader view of literacy encompassing all media (New London Group, 1996). There is some discussion whether different forms of literacy are subsumed within the overarching concept of information literacy (as in Johnston and Webber, 2003), whether it is called digital literacy or whether these are all aspects of multiliteracies.

Rather than continuing a lengthy discussion of definitions, we agree with Bawden (2001). He concludes that name and exact definitions matter rather less than a recognition that 'to deal with the complexities of the current information environment, a complex and broad form of literacy must be required', which must 'be actively promoted as a central core of the principles and practice of information science' (Bawden, 2001, 251).

Teaching information skills

When we wrote this book we thought carefully about the kinds of learning and teaching events that our readers would be involved in. We are aware that some of you will be teaching on credit-bearing information literacy programmes, while others will be offering an informal tutorial at an enquiry desk. We have a tacit knowledge of what we mean by information skills, a knowledge which it can be difficult to articulate completely.

In our view information skills relate to what Bawden describes in the paragraph above – everything to do with library and information science. Sometimes we teach people how to use a library, including even the most basic elements like how to borrow a book. At other times we teach learners about the structure of knowledge in specific subject disciplines, advanced information retrieval and knowledge management.

To put the definitions into perspective, we will now describe four different scenarios of information skills teaching. The descriptions below do not cover all the possible dimensions that will influence how we teach information skills: we have omitted number of learners, group size, gender and age for a start. What the scenarios do illustrate, however, is the variety of kinds of learning and teaching opportunities that we create or facilitate.

Digital learning

This is high-tech, content-filled teaching and learning. Learners experience a rich and complex online information environment, through which they navigate themselves. Learners are confident, networked and distributed. Much of the learning takes place through using online learning packages and completing computer-based assessment. Many resources are available online, often within the virtual learning environment. Many different forms of technology are used, ranging from digital video, online resources, interactive tutorials to discussion and chat. Feedback is generalized and always technologically mediated. Opportunities for exploration and discovery are limitless. As a teacher your role is as a guide, structuring independent learning and the acquisition of knowledge in an online environment. When we plan and develop our web pages and online learning tutorials we often imagine a content-rich learning environment, digital resources at our fingertips, and the will and competence to explore it.

Virtual learning community

This is also mediated by technology, but the focus is quite different, with a greater emphasis on online discussion, the exchange of ideas and individualized learning support. Resources are available online, but they are designed and structured so as to provide maximum feedback at every level and stage. Individual learners work with each other to produce collaborative work and the tutor is active in leading, guiding and supporting the learners' experiences. If additional support is needed there is a live chat facility where pressing concerns can be discussed and problems solved immediately. The focus of the experience is on peer and collaborative learning, on learning through action and reflection, and feedback and support. At the crudest level when we exchange e-mail conversations with an individual or groups of learners we are supporting virtual learning.

Resource-based learning

This approach is not necessarily dependent on technology (although it does not exclude it). Learners work through packages of learning material, often independently. These may be in the form of resource guides, workbooks or even just reading lists. The learners use reading and independent study to acquire their knowledge. As a tutor you have two roles: to plan and specify the resources that learners must use, and to steer or prompt the learners to their discovery of the key issues or help them to structure their understanding. This is an extreme description of traditional university education: you have a task and you work out yourself how you will get there.

Supportive learning

This is an intensive approach, not necessarily dependent on technology and often working face-to-face with a learner. The learner seeks out the teacher for help and support. This may be in the form of a supportive tutorial where as the teacher you ask the learner questions and help him or her to reach understanding, often through targeted and sensitive interventions. You will take the learning very slowly, asking for feedback from the learner at every opportunity and not moving on until you are sure the learner is ready. We often provide this kind of learning support at the information desk or when working with small groups of adult learners, but it is a universal practice, and sometimes the most rewarding.

It is clear that, given this diversity of experience, in exploring how to plan, deliver and evaluate learning and teaching experiences we need to focus on principles rather than give you instructions.

The organization of this book

The main body of this book is organized into three parts, starting with the learner, moving on to the design and delivery of learning and teaching events, and concluding by stepping back from direct learner interaction to consider evaluation and the management of learning and teaching activities.

We adopted this structure because we felt that it best represented a model for reflective and learner-centred practice, which in fact mirrored the stages that we go through in planning any form of learning and teaching event.

Section 1: Start with the learner

A great proportion of our involvement in learning and teaching activities is in the form of informal and small group teaching and the facilitation of learning. This occurs at the enquiry desk in all academic libraries and the same role is extending into other kinds of library and information organizations. We must not view learners as blank canvasses ready to accept our colouring and interpretation. In order to make learning effective we must understand something of learning and motivation in principle and also how we might find out about the learners in order to meet their needs.

Yet it is impossible to design every single learning opportunity so it exactly matches your learners' preferred learning styles. It would also be inappropriate to try to do this; in order to succeed in life we need to be flexible learners and following evolutionary theory, those who cannot adapt, do not thrive. Nevertheless we point out that being sensitive to the range of learning styles and preferences and ensuring that you try to find ways of accommodating diversity in your teaching will have benefits for all.

We also need to consider the motivations of our learners. We might fantasize that we are all such gifted and charismatic teachers that we are able to engage and inspire even the most resistant learner. This is rarely the case. We need to be conscious of the factors that will motivate and demotivate our learners. This can work at a number of levels. For example, with some groups of students, relating what you are doing to assessment can be an extremely potent motivator. Another group of learners might be interested in the subject itself and would be more motivated the more wide-ranging the content.

Theories of learning and motivation work on more abstract levels, providing a framework in which you can apply what you learn from the auditing process. Auditing in our sense means finding out about the learners and the other stakeholder groups with whom you will work. This process can range from a simple conversation or series of questions to more systematic approaches like training needs analysis.

Remember, though, that if we wish to be learner-centred in our practice, we must start with the learner and recognize his or her needs, expectations and experiences.

Section 2: Creating an effective learning and teaching experience

The middle three chapters start with the processes of planning a learning and teaching event. We explore how you can make your teaching more effective by clarifying your aims and objectives and identifying learning outcomes. This process of clarification helps learner and teacher alike. Students realize what they are going to learn and the whole of the learning and teaching experience can be aligned to meet the learning outcomes, which may themselves have been modified through negotiation with the learners. As a teacher you are able to focus on what is necessary rather than just hope for the best.

We then look at delivery – the methods and approaches you can use in teaching. To a large extent you will develop experience in using these through practice rather than reading about them, but a description of the range of alternatives available to you is still helpful. In this chapter we have supplied four case studies exemplifying the range of options you have for delivery.

Formal and informal assessment comes next. In our argument, the only way to test whether your learners have attained the learning outcomes is through assessing them. We describe the great variety of assessment methods available, and describe how they might be applied.

Section 3: Evaluation and management

Good teaching does not finish at the close of the session. It is important to stand back and look at your work. This must be achieved in a number of ways. First of all it is important to get feedback from your learners and to identify ways of evaluating that feedback.

Secondly, you must see your work of teaching and supporting learning not as something that you just go out and do but as an activity that should be nurtured, managed and reviewed. Our teaching input is rarely sustained, and we are not always in a position to gain the volume of experience that full-time teachers and trainers will acquire. This does not mean that our input will be any less professional, and in Chapter 9 we suggest some ways in which you might think about how to build a teaching team, both within your department and through alliances with other colleagues.

A last word

Finally, a summary of the purpose of this book is: Learning is learning, wherever it happens; teaching is teaching, whoever does it. You just have to do it well.

And, we hope, this book will help all who read it to do it better.

2 Learners and learning styles

Student motivation and creating the right conditions for effective learning are at the heart of this book. Later chapters will explore how as a teacher you can shape the learning experience but in this and the next chapter we will focus on learners, learning and motivation in theory and practice.

Anecdotally, one of the most distinctive features of the teaching undertaken by information professionals is that we work with strangers. We might run a single workshop for a group of people, do some impromptu coaching from an enquiry desk or produce open or online learning materials for a general and perhaps diverse target group. We work from professional assumptions of neutrality, of open and fair access to all and support and advice to everyone. This can result in a lack of focus in our activities, and perhaps even insensitivity to the particular needs of learners, especially when we have just one chance to get through to them.

By the end of this chapter we hope that you will understand some of the ideas that underpin educational and psychological theories about learners and learning. We will also link the theory to practical suggestions and case studies to illustrate how you might apply these theories to develop your practice as a teacher.

Understanding learning

There are many theories about learning and a good definition from Barker is that it involves 'permanent or temporary change in behaviour or knowledge that arises in consequence of internal or external stimulus' (Barker, 1998, 7). This contains several important ideas:

- Learning involves change.
- Change may be permanent or temporary.
- Behaviour and/or knowledge may be affected (and some people suggest we should talk about changing values as well).
- Learning may be in response to internal stimulus (you learn by yourself).
- Learning may be in response to external stimulus (shaped by a teacher or a learning experience).

It is also proposed that the learning happens on different cognitive levels. The easiest way to explain this is by looking at perhaps the best-known framework of educational objectives, 'Bloom's taxonomy'. *The Taxonomy of Educational Objectives* (Bloom, 1956) aspired to 'provide a classification of the goals of our educational system' and has been applied to assess learning outcomes and define the nature of learning ever since. Though the work has its critics, it is a helpful definition of the outcomes of learning. According to the classification there are three domains of learning – cognitive, affective and psychomotor. Each domain consists of several levels. So the cognitive domain consists of:

- Knowledge
- Comprehension
- Application
- Analysis
- Synthesis
- Evaluation.

The affective domain consists of:

- Receiving
- Responding
- Valuing

- Organizing and conceptualizing
- Characterizing by value or value concept.

The work on the psychomotor domain was never completed. We will discuss applications of Bloom's taxonomy in Chapter 5.

Very few people are perfect autodidacts. Nearly all of us need teachers to shape our learning and help us to make sense of new material. The teacher is not just someone who lectures in a classroom, but a person who shapes and guides our way to new knowledge and understanding. As we will explore in later chapters, this can be in formal and informal surroundings, face-to-face or using open or online learning materials.

But before we progress, just a pause for thought. Within the library and information world do we perhaps assume that the only barriers to autonomous and independent learning are information skills and knowledge? Unconsciously we believe that once individuals possess information skills and become information literate, they will be effective learners. Yet our assumption runs contrary to much learning theory. Many educational theories are built on principles of active teacher intervention and the structured creation of learning opportunities. The ways in which libraries and information-gathering support and enhance learning are little considered, and we rest many of our professional values on universal, seamless access to the information universe.

So we start with a contradiction, and one that applies to much of our teaching: on one hand there is a core professional value of universal access to information, on the other structured teaching of what is relevant. We can identify ways of applying current theories of learning and teaching to our work in the practice of teaching and learning support, yet there is often limited appreciation of the fundamental purpose of what we do.

You might find it useful to think about the theme of this chapter by reflecting on the way you approach learning. In *The Lecturer's Toolkit* Race and Brown (1998) ask readers to think of:

- something you are good at, and how you became good at it
- something about yourself you feel good about and your evidence for this positive feeling

- something you do not feel positive about and why this is the case
- something you learnt successfully, against the odds.

This practical activity is used to build a very clear description of the influences on learning. In a later work, Race and Brown (2001) summarize them into five factors:

- Wanting to learn (or intrinsic motivation). Not all learners demonstrate this. For every motivated family historian there is a disaffected youth who falls asleep in class. It can be possible to find ways of engaging most learners through effective planning and design.
- Needing to learn (or extrinsic motivation). The most obvious example here is when learners need the skills or knowledge to pass an assessment.
- Learning by doing. Active learning is generally believed to be more motivating, especially with adult learners.
- Learning from feedback. Let the learners find out how they are doing.
- Making sense of what has been learned. Developing understanding must be at the heart of teaching. Anything else is just training or passing on information.

In practical terms, in order to motivate your learners you need to identify ways of maximizing each of these five influences. Some of this will be through the way you design the learning opportunity and the techniques you use; another part will be what the learners bring to the experience; and a final element will be the way you can respond to the learners.

And yet what do we know about how people learn – and why different people like to learn in quite different ways? There is a vast and sometimes contradictory literature on these areas, and in the next section we will explore some of those themes very briefly.

Theories of learning

Many theories are used to explain how people learn. Often the theories are based on quite different assumptions about human nature and society.

Although most teachers unconsciously use a mixture of these theories, we thought it would be illuminating to consider them in order to reflect on what they mean in terms of the values that they bring to the design of learning activities.

If you wish to read more about this see the suggestions for further reading at the end of the book. A good starting point is the text by Jarvis, Holford and Griffin (1998), which provides a helpful summary and review of most of these approaches, and James Atherton's websites (2003).

Behaviourism

The focus of learning according to this school of thought is a change in behaviour. The foundations of behaviourism are Pavlov's work conditioning dogs to salivate on hearing a bell that they had been conditioned to associate with food, and the research of Frederic Skinner. Skinner demonstrated that the behaviour of rats and pigeons could be shaped through the provision of reward in the form of food, described as 'positive reinforcement'.

Behaviourism has two main influences on current learning and teaching practice. The first is in the increasingly popular focus on problem-solving or learning by trial and error with the teacher intervening to provide either positive or negative reinforcement – or encourage or dissuade the learners' decisions or directions. Much legal and, increasingly, medical education is based around these approaches, in the UK at least, and often law information skills training starts with a problem that the learners need to research. The second behaviourist approach is instrumental teaching, which aims to change learner behaviour without changing knowledge or values. This is used to great effect in some therapy, particularly in aversion therapy, but it can be inappropriate in much information skills teaching. For example, a common mistake is focusing on behaviour modification rather than developing knowledge or understanding, so you train people to use a database 'correctly' but give them no understanding of why this method of using the database is correct and what benefits it will bring.

Cognitivist theories

Cognitivist theories deal with the way that awareness of the outside world is internalized either through assimilation (or fitting the ideas into your mind) or accommodation (by changing your existing knowledge or understanding). Probably the best-known cognitivist is Jean Piaget, whose research on children proposed a stage theory of mental development starting with infants developing sensory motor skills to the development of abstract thought in teenagers (Piaget, 1950).

A second cognitivist researcher has become increasingly influential. Lev Vygotsky (1978) discusses two concepts: the actual development level of the learner and what is called the 'zone of proximal development'. This is defined as: 'the distance between the actual developmental level as determined by independent problem-solving and the level of potential development as determined through problem-solving under adult guidance or in collaboration with more capable peers' (Vygotsky, 1978).

The emphasis on potential rather than achievement led to an increased role for supported learning, using techniques like scaffolding (which we will discuss later), group work, guidance and coaching. Vygotsky also writes about the importance of affective learning, how learning changes your emotions or values, ideas that we will return to in Chapter 6.

Vygotsky's ideas of extending learning potential through effective support can provide some of the most powerful pedagogic justifications for librarian input into information skills or information literacy training, and an inspiring framework for the design of learning and teaching strategies.

Social learning

Social learning is a blanket term used by Jarvis, Holford and Griffin (1998) when they discuss the influence of sociology and social psychology on learning theory: we exist in society and therefore learn within it. Our learning is naturally conditioned by our environment, be it our national culture, gender expectations, social class or immediate peer group. There is a strong Darwinian influence, with much discussion of how groups respond to society and grow, change or evolve to survive. Key theorists of social learning are Mead (1950) and Bandura (1977, 1986). In terms of teaching in practice, these theories raise the importance of the environment at micro and macro level, and emphasize how teachers might shape the environment to influence the learning experience.

Although not linked to social learning theorists, there is an interesting parallel in the authors' experience of contextualized skills teaching, which we discussed briefly in Chapter 1.

Experiential learning

Experiential learning takes learners' experiences (which can be actively constructed or created for the purpose) and turns them into learning. This process is most widely known through Kolb's learning cycle (Figure 2.1, Kolb, 1984). The principle is that ideas are formed and re-formed through a cycle of experience.

The learning process starts with concrete experience; then learners must have time to reflect on what they have learnt before drawing up theories and processing the new ideas through 'abstract conceptualization'. During the final stage, 'active experimentation', learners use the theories they have drawn up to test and solve problems. Kolb's learning cycle is an iterative process that describes learning not only as the process of receiving information and converting it to knowledge, but also emphasizes the importance of reflection and action.

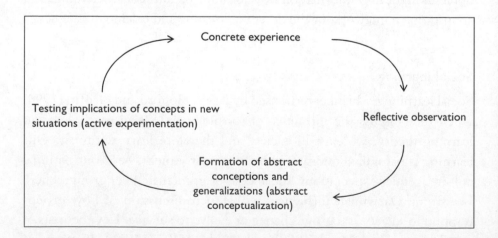

Figure 2.1 Kolb's experiential learning cycle

Experiential learning approaches are often used when working with adults and Kolb's learning cycle can be a very powerful way of structuring a learning and teaching event. However, plan your starting point carefully: imagine starting a session with a group of technophobic learners by asking for stories about their experiences of using a computer. Rather start by asking for experiences of how they have found information before!

Another way of doing this is within a practical session, where the learners are asked to reflect on what they have done, and then to practise ways of refining their searches. This can be a very effective approach when looking at internet searching. You can use the experiences of the group of learners, perhaps by asking about search engines they have used and why, and then go on to demonstrate, explain and practise how to use more advanced search techniques.

Constructivism

Constructivism draws from the last three approaches. The underlying assumption of constructivism is that learners do not absorb knowledge passively, but rather construct their learning on the basis of prior knowledge and experiences. Learning is more effective if learners are encouraged to try out and test what they have learned through problem-solving. Biggs' (2003) book is perhaps the most persuasive advocate of this approach.

Constructivists create dynamic and interactive learning communities with the tutor influencing and shaping the learning experience. As a teaching approach it is very powerful, defining a teaching experience that is about much more than information transmission. Many online learning environments are based on constructivist approaches, designing a rich learning universe of content, activity and interaction within the same virtual space.

However, it can sometimes seem as if so much is designed into constructivist approaches that there is little space for independent and self-regulated learning, and certainly no space for someone just going to a library and reading beyond the identified material.

Summary

We have explored how effective learning is concerned with:

- behaviour modification
- personal development
- social context
- experience
- design.

A synthesis of these five sets of theories defines our understanding of how learning takes place, but this is only part of the learning equation. We must next consider influences on the learner, and in particular personality and culture.

Personality and learning

Think back to Race and Brown's questions at the beginning of this chapter: how did you learn to do something well? The way the learning was designed might have been important, but another element in your learning might be your personality and culture. If you recognize this, then it follows that your students learn in ways that reflect their personalities and cultures. Acknowledging that not everyone will learn in the same way can be a powerful key to understanding how to motivate learners. Even more useful is having an awareness of the different ways in which people might like to learn.

The way someone learns is often described as a learning style, but what we actually mean by that definition can vary. Curry (1983, 1990) provides a much-cited and very helpful classification of learning styles relating to:

- personality type (for example introverts and extroverts)
- information-processing preference
- instructional preference.

Following Curry, a learning style may be described as the strategy that you adopt when learning, or it might be your cognitive style for learning –

whether your learning style is innate or a response to external forces. Some of these strategies and styles are discussed below.

Learning strategies

Deep and surface learning

A surface approach is a utilitarian approach to assessment where learners will adapt their learning to match the requirements of the course, simply regurgitating the information required, but not retaining the new knowledge for any length of time. Deep learning takes place when learners absorb or digest the new information. In terms of information-seeking behaviours and characteristics, remember that for much of the time in your information skills sessions you will be aiming to achieve some fundamental change in the ways that your learners approach information research or use. Most of us have been deep and surface learners, depending on our motivation and the circumstances, but some strategies are suggested in later chapters for developing deep learning. There is another approach called strategic or achieving learning in which you plan your learning to get good marks but you might ignore the underlying purpose of the task.

Holistic and serialist learning

Serialist learners work step by step in a linear way, usually only pulling together a complete picture at the end. Holistic learners try to put a whole picture together at the start and fit the details in later. They may work in quite haphazard ways. Setting activities to work through piece by piece would work well with serialist learners, but would be less comfortable for holistic learners. A holistic learner might prefer topic-based learning or the freedom to explore on his or her own within an overall area (Pask, 1976).

Cognitive styles for learning

Kolb's experiential learning style

Kolb's description of the learning cycle is also translated into individual learning styles, starting along two axes. The first dimension relates to whether you are a concrete or an abstract thinker. This means whether you think in terms of real things or events or are drawn to ideas and theory. The second dimension relates to whether information is processed in an active or reflective way. The two dimensions combine to form four different learning styles:

- *Diverger* You think in concrete terms and process what you learn reflectively. You need to be personally engaged in the learning activity.
- *Converger* You perceive information abstractly and process it reflectively. You need to follow detailed sequential steps in a learning activity.
- *Assimilator* You think in abstractions and process your new knowledge actively in the company of others. You would need to be involved in pragmatic problem solving in a learning activity.
- *Accommodator* You think in concrete terms and process information actively. You need to be involved in risk taking, making changes, experimentation and flexibility.

Honey and Mumford

Honey and Mumford (1992) applied Kolb's theories approach in a widely used questionnaire, which describes four different learning styles most often applied to management development:

- *Activists* respond best to learning situations offering challenges, and enjoy new experiences, excitement and freedom in their learning – 'learning by doing something new'.
- *Pragmatists* like relevant learning opportunities with scope for theory and practice – 'learning what is useful'.
- *Reflectors* prefer structured learning opportunities that provide time to step back and observe, reflect and think about what has happened. They often seek out detail – 'learning through reflection'.
- *Theorists* like logical, rational structure, clear aims and the opportunity to question and analyse what they have learnt – 'learning from theory'.

Gardner's theory of multiple intelligences

Gardner (1983) used biological as well as cultural research to formulate a theory of multiple intelligences, which are:

- logical–mathematical – to detect patterns, reason deductively and think logically
- linguistic – to use language to express oneself and to remember information verbally
- spatial – to manipulate and create mental images in order to solve problems
- musical – to recognize and compose musical pitches, tones and rhythms
- bodily kinesthetic – to co-ordinate bodily movements
- interpersonal and intrapersonal – to understand your own feelings and intentions and those of others.

According to this theory all intelligences are required and it is important to find ways of supporting and developing them all, unlike traditional education which has favoured logical–mathematical and linguistic intelligence most of all. Everyone has different strengths in each of these, and the level of these intelligences will often determine preferred learning styles.

VARK (www.vark-learn.com)

This stands for Visual, Aural, Read/Write and Kinesthetic. This style for learning starts from the assumption that people have a preferred sense, which dominates the way information is processed. If you have a visual preference, you learn best from seeing, if kinesthetic you learn from activity.

Using these theories in teaching

Rayner and Riding (1997) suggest that all these theories can be classified on two axes:

- *Wholist–analytic* – whether you organize information into wholes or parts
- *Verbal–imagery* – whether you represent information by thinking in words or in images.

In practice, the important principle to remember from these theories is that you should always try to provide a mix of teaching and learning activities in order to accommodate diversity. For example, try to include activity, theory, thinking space and relevant examples in a session, and do not just talk through examples, but illustrate them with a handout that includes diagrams or a visual representation of what you are covering; allow plenty of time for practice.

This is also a consideration if you want to make your teaching inclusive, so that a learner who is dyslexic would gain as much benefit from the learning experience as anyone else. Inclusive learning and teaching should accommodate people with many different needs through good planning and design.

Culture and gender

Many texts and guides about teaching are rooted in a specific national context, even if this is not discussed explicitly. But if you work with learners from more than one country, you realize very quickly that each nationality has quite different experiences and expectations. In short, people come from diverse national cultures that influence how they approach learning and how you can motivate them. Gender and education is also a topic of concern: do boys and girls (or men and women) learn differently?

One of the most interesting overviews of the differences between national cultures is Geert Hofstede's book *Culture's Consequences* (2001). The author argues that people have different values depending on their country of origin. Different national cultures are defined using five dimensions:

- *Power distance* – the extent to which less powerful members of organizations and institutions accept and expect that power be distributed unequally.

- *Uncertainty avoidance* – how comfortable or uncomfortable people feel in unstructured situations.
- *Individualism and collectivism* – whether people look after themselves or remain integrated into groups, particularly the family.
- *Masculinity and femininity* – tough masculine, traditionalist cultures compared with tender feminine societies.
- *Long-term versus short-term orientation* – the extent to which people accept delayed gratification of material, social and emotional needs.

The first four dimensions offer some very useful insights into working with students and teachers from different cultures.

Power distance

Power distance is really about how much control and respect is accorded to someone in authority. In a country with a low power distance index (PDI) teachers will treat students as equals, education itself is described as student-centred and education is seen a two-way process between students and the expert teacher. This is a clear description of the British educational system, certainly at university level if not before. In a country with a high PDI (like China and other Far Eastern countries) students are dependent on teachers who are seen as gurus able to transfer personal wisdom. Teachers initiate all communication in class and demand respect and authority. Equally, students from China and other high PDI countries are not accustomed to asking questions or disagreeing with the teacher, yet if they come to study in the UK, Australasia or North America, this is just what they are expected to do.

Uncertainty avoidance

Hofstede argues that the level of uncertainty avoidance in a culture has a profound effect on the nature of teaching. In Germany and France, countries with a strong uncertainty avoidance index (UAI), students and teachers favour structured learning. Timetables and precise learning outcomes are valued. In countries with a lower uncertainty avoidance index, like the UK, learning is seen as an open-ended process or as a dialogue seeking originality and debate. Hofstede even suggests that this influences academic discourse. In low UAI countries intellectual disagreement is valued, unconventionality tolerated, and conveying complex ideas in simple language is a mark of an expert. He contrasts this with high UAI countries where academic language is impenetrable, rules are more prescriptive and there are intellectual absolutes. In practical terms, this might mean that you should think about how you structure a session, and possibly even how you demonstrate your command of the material you will be covering.

Individualism and collectivism

The USA, Australia and Canada are all examples of individualist societies. In these cultures personal opinions are valued, conflict is expected and students are encouraged to speak up. Study groups might form, but usually only in order to do a task. In collectivist societies (including Latin American and many Asian countries), harmony reigns supreme, and the group comes first. If a teacher wishes students to speak in class, each one must be addressed directly. Groups based on ethnic origin establish themselves and stay together.

Masculinity and femininity

Masculinity and femininity are classifications relating to the relative importance of social goals (like relationships, helping others), which are defined as feminine, compared with the masculine ego goals of career and money. In masculine societies (like Japan, the UK and the USA) academic failure is unacceptable. Awards and public praise for excellence are highly valued. In feminine countries (including Scandinavia and the Netherlands) weak students are encouraged and often students will be self-effacing about their own performance. They may even appear to be less motivated if you use measures that have been developed in the USA or the UK (Bråten and Olaussen, 2000). In an information skills context, think about what impact this might have if you asked students to assess their own knowledge or performance. If you had Dutch and English students would the results be immediately comparable?

Even if you are not convinced by Hofstede's theories, they can offer useful starting points to reflect on whether you have particular expectations of the ways your learners should behave, and whether there may be cultural or gender differences. Even in very simple things like attitudes to timekeeping, you will find quite major differences between learners from Africa and North America, so it is critical to be aware of this before passing judgement on the motivation or abilities of your learners.

Experience and expectation

Most learning theories suggest that 'the way people perceive a learning task 'is partly determined by his or her previous experience' (Franken, 1998). Or, remembering Piaget, people will process information into some consistency with existing categories, beliefs, attitudes, values, stereotypes and behaviour. Cottrell reinforces this by stating that 'most of us develop frameworks that inhibit learning usually based on previous experiences of learning' (Cottrell, 2001).

Imagine what the last idea means when you are teaching information skills. A student who has been sent along for a 'library session' might have particular expectations. In a university context, many students start with the assumption that as public or school library users and already internet-savvy, there will be little to learn in an information skills class. What effect will that have on their motivation? Equally, how could you challenge these assumptions?

Learning technologies and modes of learning

To what extent do different learning technologies, or the shift to distance learning affect the way that you learn? This is a very complex question, to which answers are as yet unproven.

The assumption in this book is that different learning technologies do not have a fundamental influence on the nature of teaching, but will influence your choice of methods and techniques. Whatever the context, the principles of effective pedagogy remain constant. Nevertheless different modes of learning offer some challenges if you are used to working in more traditional face-to-face contexts. These include:

- *Time* Online learning may be either synchronous – the learning event happens in real time, like an online discussion or videoconferencing – or asynchronous. Even in asynchronous mode you can still create timetables and interaction through e-mail discussion, establishing group tasks, and so on.
- *Groups and individuals* Online and distance learning can be a way of building learning communities through communication and groupwork but also very isolating – one person at a computer or working in a study.
- *Delivery of content* One of the key differences with online and paper-based distance learning material is that much of the content needs to be developed before the learners start the course, and producing online learning materials takes time.

We will discuss some of the key theories of e-learning from Laurillard and Salmon in Chapter 5.

Learning and learning styles in practice

It would be impossible to make provision for every mix of learning styles and learning strategies in every bit of teaching you ever do. Nevertheless, there are some approaches that you can adopt that might make your learning and teaching event more comfortable for all your learners.

- *Variety and variation* Plan how you can use a mixture of teaching techniques within your class. It can be helpful to think of ways of breaking your session into 20-minute blocks of time, and then changing what you do in each block. This might be by following an explanation with a hands-on practical, or by setting different kinds of practical work, or simply by changing the pace of what you do. In an online environment think about times when you can use group and individual activities, alternating group discussion with individual tasks, or how you can vary the activities. Try to reinforce messages in more than one medium. Rather than just saying the name of a database, write it down or show it to people. Use screen shots and diagrams as well as plain text to explain your meaning, and give people time to practise.

- *Study skills and learning skills* Some research (see Cottrell, 2001) suggests that 'learning to learn' programmes can be very effective. This evidence can be used to justify information professional input into teaching and training events. Even if you modify this conclusion by recognizing that the skills need to be rooted within a subject context, it is still an evidence-based rationale for formal information skills programmes.

- *Your teaching persona* Recognizing your own preferred cognitive style should make you more sensitive to how you like to teach and what assumptions you have about learning and learners. You do not need to be a chameleon to be an effective teacher. But if you are an abstract thinker you might need to pin your examples down when working with adult learners.

Case study 1   Library induction for international students

Every year Cliff and a colleague run a library induction and skills session for a group of postgraduate students on an international MA. Students spend one term at their university and the next two terms in Switzerland and Italy, respectively. Competition to do the course is fierce and most students give up well paid jobs to come and do the programme and are highly motivated to do well on the course, but are also keen to network and build links that will influence their future careers.

Students have to use the library and electronic resources in order to complete their assignments, so they all need to reach the same level of knowledge and confidence.

The greatest challenge to teaching information skills is the diversity of the group. Out of a class of 25 there will usually be at least 17 nationalities, from every continent. This has two main consequences. First, the students will have very different expectations of university education, libraries and electronic resources. Imagine the different experiences of someone who studied at an elite US college, compared with those from Russia, Bhutan, China or Colombia. Secondly, the students behave in very different ways. Some students are very talkative, others will not speak, some take the whole induction very seriously, others do not. There is no collective norm for behaviour.

What happens in the session?

Cliff and his colleague run the session together, with the hope that a higher staff–student ratio will make it easier to manage the students. The session is a mixture of talk, demo, tour and practical, with a structured worksheet to reinforce the rest of the content.

During the tour some of the students talk all the time and then anarchy reigns during the hands-on element. Some diligently work through the practical, others go directly onto Hotmail or do their own internet searching, while a few try to disappear to have a cup of coffee or play football. Some students request lots of assistance, others have no tolerance for any delay or uncertainty while others ask no questions and work on their own.

At the end of the session Cliff and his colleague have to go and sit down for a rest. Feedback from the students is always positive, but is the session effective and what else could they do?

Questions

1. What comments would you make about the approach to induction and information skills adopted by Cliff and his colleague?
2. How would you approach teaching information skills to this group?
3. What other approaches could you adopt in working with such a diverse group?

Discussion

Cliff and his colleague are trying to do too much in their session and that makes it seem chaotic. Ideally they would probably divide their session into two – one a straightforward library induction and the second a more comprehensive information skills session. They might also try to divide up the group by level of experience and make the session more focused.

However, this does not mean that the session would be guaranteed to run more smoothly. Cliff has already adopted some good strategies for dealing with the diverse group, including auditing their needs and experiences, using team teaching so that there is a good staff–student ratio, and providing structured handouts and active learning opportunities. Given the constraints of the students' timetable and his own resources at the start of the academic year this seems a reasonable approach, which would meet the desired learning outcomes.

Case study 2   Inclusive teaching and learning support

In the UK it is estimated that about 2% of university students are dyslexic, although the proportion at any specific institution varies. Dyslexia is a broad spectrum disorder, and differs in its exact nature and intensity from individual to individual. In general people with dyslexia have difficulty with linear thought and processing text. They can struggle to gain information from texts and may have problems with spelling, grammar, reading speed and structuring their writing. At the same time they often have strengths in other areas, including spoken communication and lateral thinking, and are just as intelligent as any other student.

After being assessed by an educational psychologist, a dyslexic student may qualify for additional funding, which will allow for the purchase of specialist equipment and covers photocopying costs and sometimes even pays for an assistant. The educational psychologist's report includes advice on ways of studying with dyslexia, and this can make a constructive starting point when discussing learner support needs.

Some students do not discover they have dyslexia until they have reached university (or even enter their final year). This means that along with all of the normal life-stage transitions that happen when you leave home, start to live independently and begin studying in a new and strange environment, dyslexic students have to come to terms with being identified as dyslexic.

Most new students are daunted by the university library: the size and scale are usually very different from the school, college or public libraries they used, and the way that they will be expected to use libraries as autonomous learners is different from before. Sometimes the students are given a topic and told to go and find academic material on it: no reading list, just a requirement that their subject matter comes from verified academic sources.

For people with dyslexia the culture shock is magnified. The size of the bookstock and the length of the shelves can be alarming. Even worse, the classification system and the strange sequences can be totally disorienting. Sometimes tutors do not make life any easier, for example by giving students oral rather than written instructions. It can be very stressful to research artists when you don't know how to spell their names! Additionally some dyslexic people have problems with self-organization and time management, so they struggle to remember appointments and the due dates of books, which can easily lead to problems with overdue books and fines.

Jane is as an academic librarian supporting students with additional needs, both through one-to-one contact and through service development. She is working with increasing numbers of dyslexic students, often referred to her directly by the disability unit, although a few come to see her without direct referral.

Questions

1. How aware are you of the differing requirements of your learner groups?
2. What kinds of things do you think Jane should do?

Discussion

Jane's work to support these learners works at a variety of levels:

- individualized one-to-one support
- development of library services
- networking within the institution
- staff development.

Jane is very aware that she needs to understand the specific needs of individual learners in order to support them most effectively. Equally, she must find ways to develop their information skills so they can use the library independently if possible while feeling that support is available whenever required. When students come to see Jane they sit down and talk through what they need.

Even in these informal situations Jane is aware that she is teaching, combining her knowledge of dyslexia with her skills in structuring learning opportunities to change behaviour or increase knowledge. She must help her learners find ways to overcome barriers.

She might start her work with a student by running a personalized induction session. Even when the student has attended one of the general library induction sessions, Jane finds that she needs to spend several hours over a few days covering library essentials, perhaps taking the students on a tour or going over the same material more than once to improve understanding. She uses mindmaps and diagrams to help explain points, as dyslexic people are often more comfortable with visual representations of ideas.

Jane helps learners to find coping strategies to make the most of the library. This includes ways to use the OPAC more effectively, for example using keyword rather than title searches, browsing rather than searching the indexes, and helping students to use specialist software to check their OPAC entries. Journals are particularly problematic, since some students have difficulties in understanding what they are, let alone how they are arranged. Electronic journals and article references add even more layers of complexity!

Jane also helps students to use the most complicated databases, showing them how to set up more helpful interfaces by changing screen magnification or working with some of the specialist software available. She may refer learners to the subject librarians, but sometimes she will broker the enquiries because the students prefer to work with someone they already know.

Library services have adjusted to the needs of learners with additional needs. In particular students who are dyslexic are offered extended loans. In addition Jane might negotiate with the lending section over fines and overdue books. Specialist software like Inspiration (for organizing and presenting information), Read and Write (reads text and assists with the composition of written material) and Wordswork (study skills) are also available within the library so that students can be comfortable studying in the library and have access to specialist support. There have also been some attempts to develop library stock so that more talking books are available and that signage and guiding is effective for all learners, not just aesthetically appealing.

Networking with colleagues within the institution is important. Part of this is because so many learners visit Jane after referral from other central departments and she needs to be in regular contact with other staff to confirm that students are eligible for the additional services. In addition Jane needs to understand what is happening outside the department in order to get a rounded picture of the student experience, and she finds that her other work as an academic librarian (carrying out induction training, teaching, enquiry work and academic liaison) supports her day-to-day work with her specific student groups. Her links also raise the profile of the library more widely within the institution, and demonstrate that libraries and librarians are actively involved in supporting learning, not just in providing access to resources.

Another element of Jane's work is to advise her library colleagues about ways of making their teaching and learner support more sensitive to the needs of students with dyslexia. This is a very general description and ranges from increasing awareness of student needs among front-line staff to giving guidelines for teaching.

Teaching development is focused on adopting inclusive approaches, since what helps learners with additional needs actually works for everyone. By inclusive approaches we mean finding ways that do not disadvantage particular groups, which in practice means using a mixture of teaching styles and delivery approaches. Jane reminds people not just to show learners databases, but to give them handouts to reinforce the information they provide, and to give learners the opportunity to practise their learning in hands-on sessions.

Jane has drawn up some internal guidelines for the provision of written material. They recommend that all materials are printed in a sans-serif font, preferably of 12-point or greater size, and printed on coloured paper (cream by preference). Research findings suggest that this makes text easier to read.

Finally, when you look at the description of the strategies Jane adopts in her informal work with learners it is clear that many of them could be used in any kind of teaching situation. Tours, personalized support and a clear understanding of learner needs are relevant to all kinds of learning and teaching environments.

3 Motivating learners

In the previous chapter we explored some of the most helpful theories of learning in terms of pedagogic design and individual and cultural differences. In this more practical chapter we will concentrate on how you can use this knowledge to enhance the motivation of your learners. The topic of motivation is linked closely to the theme of the next chapter, auditing, finding out about your learners' needs and prior experiences – since understanding something about your learners will influence the way you design any learning and teaching activity or event.

What is motivation?

The assumption behind any discussion of motivation is that there is a cause for every form of behaviour. Franken (1998) classifies theories of motivation in three groups, as shown in Table 3.1.

Table 3.1 Theories of motivation

Theory	Underpinning assumptions
Biological	Evolutionary and genetic drive for survival
Learning	Environment, culture, personal learning and development shape behaviour
Cognitive	Mental representations guide behaviour

In our context the last two groups of theories are more relevant than the first. We have already looked at some of the key theories of learning in Chapter 2, and we will now turn to some theories of motivation. Most texts about motivation in learning and teaching ignore general theories of motivation in the workplace (see for example the various contributors in Brown, Armstrong and Thompson, 1998), an absence that we hope to address very briefly. For further information we recommend you have a look at Mullins (2002) or Buchanan and Huczynski (2004).

The hierarchy of needs

Abraham Maslow (1954) devised a theory of human nature that proposed that everyone was motivated to satisfy a series of basic needs arranged in a hierarchy (Figure 3.1). At the most basic level the motivations were physiological – for food, drink, shelter and survival. This level was followed by a need for safety and security, including protection from physical and psychological threats. The third level was social – a need for love, belonging, trust and affection. The penultimate need was to satisfy the ego in the form of self-respect, confidence, recognition, status and power. The final level of needs was self-actualization – self-fulfilment, achievement, individual growth and motivation.

Maslow believed that individuals moved between the different levels and that once one level was fulfilled they would move on to the next level. Following this theory, the ultimate goal of teaching is self-actualization – the realization of human potential. You may find it interesting to reflect

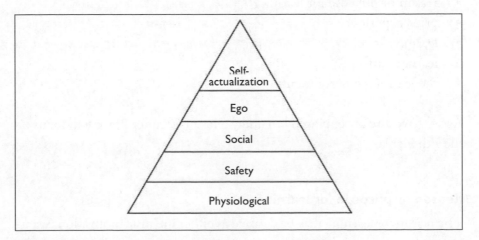

Figure 3.1 Maslow's hierarchy of needs

how you might apply the hierarchy in a classroom-based learning and teaching event!

Herzberg's hygiene factors

Herzberg (1968) proposes a two-factor theory of motivation. The first elements were described as hygiene factors, mainly with an environmental cause. The second were described as motivators. The value of Herzberg to learning and teaching practice is that the hygiene factors do not motivate, but they can demotivate. Thus the quality of your classroom will not motivate your learners, but it can demotivate them.

Achievement motivation

It is suggested that the level of motivation to achievement varies between individuals. Some people are highly driven and like to win in competitive environments; others are less highly motivated.

Learning and motivation

Motivation in learning derives from a combination of several elements:

- reason or purpose for learning
- prior experience
- learning style
- learner attitude
- the learning environment.

As we have already explored learning styles in Chapter 2, we will focus on the other areas.

Reason or purpose for learning

The reason for learning may be defined as either intrinsic motivation (wanting to learn) or extrinsic motivation (needing to learn). It is sometimes suggested that extrinsic motivation always leads to instrumental or surface learning, but this is rather unfair. You might have an extrinsic motivation to learn how to drive a car, but this does not mean that you do not do your best to learn how to be a good driver.

The decision to learn can be voluntary (as in the case of much adult learning) or compulsory (as at school). Even when people choose to learn they may be studying for quite different purposes. Someone studying for a business or IT qualification probably has career goals, whereas someone studying genealogy or art history is probably doing this mainly for personal interest. You might want to consider whether learners' reasons for learning would have any effect on the way that you approach your teaching and how you articulate your learning outcomes. For example, if you are running an induction session on a professional course, it might be reasonable to assume that your students are more interested in the usefulness and relevance of library and information resources, and would prefer a concise and business-like introduction. On the other hand you might find that it is better to focus a session for researchers on a critical approach to resources and searching techniques.

In no case should you assume that the motivation of learners is permanent. Even when someone wants to learn commitment can be challenged or reinforced by external factors like job change, peer pressure or personality and self-belief. It can sometimes appear very confusing when a learner expresses a need for one thing, and then does nothing to address that need. In some contexts that might mean anonymous survey respondents requesting staff training sessions but few actual participants, or students stating a need to find out more but not attending relevant classes or just a high attrition rate on an online course. Factors for non-attendance may have nothing to do with learners' interest in the subject, and can serve to improve or diminish motivation of all participants.

Prior experience

Adult learners in particular bring memories of previous learning experiences into each new learning event. This can create preconceptions of what the teaching and learning event will be like, and also brings misconceptions and fears – for example that they need to be an expert computer user or that they will get into trouble if they do something wrong.

There are two fairly straightforward solutions to dealing with reticence in adult learners. The first approach is to be very clear about what you are planning to do. Set clear objectives, establish ground rules and then give people the opportunity to learn at their own pace. Secondly, the development of a group ethos can help to sustain motivation and reinforce commitment, so for example if you work with an established group of part-time learners they may attend because that is what they always do, and they can support each other in their learning.

With adult learners, auditing is especially important: you must find ways of gauging their existing knowledge and expectations. We will explore this theme further in the next chapter.

Learner attitude

Much of the time learning opportunities are offered with the expectation that people are ready to learn. Thus we assume that if learners go to a class they will be ready to learn; but this is not always the case. Sometimes this can be because learners reject the content of a particular session, but there can be some more serious fundamental reasons.

Perhaps the most challenging barriers are to do with the learners' self-concept (whether they believe they have the capability to learn) and self-regulation (how they manage themselves as learners). This means that you may work with a group of people who do not believe that they will be able to do the task. This self-doubt may even manifest itself in difficult or challenging behaviour.

It is suggested (Zimmerman, 2000) that this concept of 'self-efficacy' – believing in your capability to learn – is more responsive to teacher intervention than many other personality traits. So, as a teacher, you may be able to increase the motivation of your learners through the practical approaches discussed below.

But even more difficult to address is the notion of self-regulation in learning. This might be characterized as effective personal organization for learning, by believing that you can succeed and marshalling your personal resources to meet this belief. Equally, as Järvelä and Niemivirta (1999) describe, if students think they may fail, they can intentionally create obstacles to possible achievement, so that failure cannot be attributed to a lack of ability. It could be suggested that bad behaviour in a formal classroom environment might sometimes be attributed to this. From our experience, it can be much more straightforward to motivate academically able learners (already efficacious, self-regulated and often self-selected) than learners from less straightforward backgrounds.

This whole approach becomes even more complicated when you are working with a very diverse group of learners, spanning many different sets of ability in the same group.

The learning environment

The fifth part of motivation in learning is a composite of many different elements. This umbrella term includes:

- venue
- time of day
- heat
- lighting
- furniture
- room layout
- how many computers are available (and whether the learners have to share them).

The environment may be something you are able to control – and you should make every effort to do so. Before you run a session you need to check that you have all the equipment you need, and that it is working, that the room layout is acceptable and that any visuals you use can be seen.

Equally you may not always be able to control the learning environment. There may be gremlins that cause your computer network to crash as soon as you start a session, or the heating controls break down, or more learners than expected turn up so there aren't enough seats for everyone or many other possible crises. In cases like this, remember that you do not need to carry on bravely. If the learning environment becomes too uncomfortable or awkward, just stop and send your learners away. It is better to stop a session than to make learners sit through one where equipment does not function properly.

This is another example of when your role as a 'teacher' is different from your role as an information professional. The information professional's approach is invariably to accommodate and include, but when you are running a teaching and learning event you need to remember that you are in charge and should make decisions to avoid damaging the learning experience for everyone.

Motivation and information skills

As we said in Chapter 2, most of the time teaching information skills is spent working with strangers. This can in itself create particular challenges. If you are running a course for a whole day or across a number of sessions you have much more time and space to plan your curriculum, create variety and pace in the sessions and get to know your learners as individuals. If you have no more than an hour with a group of people you have never met before, or at least never before as learners, it is much more difficult to guarantee it will all be right first time.

Often attending the course is a process of adjusting to the teacher and other learners. In the 'quick fix' information skills session you are often working with learners who:

- do not understand why they have been sent to the library/information centre/this course
- are not interested in the session because they either believe they can do it or actually might be able to do it
- see this as a distraction from their main goal or objective
- succumb to peer pressure that this sort of thing is silly
- are scared – people do not like to be told that they have been making mistakes
- present difficult or challenging behaviour
- opt out.

In later chapters we will discuss ways that you might be able to reduce some of these perceptions, but we would be misleading if we suggested that you would never encounter these sorts of behaviours and attitudes. If you talk to other teachers and trainers they will often share exactly the same experiences, even with the luxury of full academic status. The value of teaching cannot always be assessed through popular audience reaction.

Motivation in practice

Some of the ways of synthesizing theory and experience are described below.

Provide a clear rationale for the learning

You should articulate the learning outcomes or purpose of the session clearly to the group or individual. You could do this in the form of a slide or section in a handout, guide or e-learning package when you discuss the learning outcomes. However you express the rationale, let the learners know what is going to happen and how it will meet their desire or need to learn.

In face-to-face and some online learning environments, remember that you can modify your content in response to learner feedback, and do not see this as a failure but an opportunity to make your teaching more relevant. Most new teachers over-prepare, and often people working as library and information professionals never get the volume of experience that means you stop being a 'new' teacher.

Make it clear what you are doing and why, breaking the training down into separate elements. These act as signposts to the learners and help to build a common starting point, are benchmarks for progress and enable learners to make sense of a session which might cover many diverse services and themes.

You might also consider whether there are opportunities to embed the information skills work into other activities. Vidmar (1998) describes how he went to students' classrooms before they came to the library for information skills training, and this resulted in measurably more positive learner motivation.

Another option is described by Schunk (1981), who suggests that children who observed an adult work through a problem were more motivated than those who were just given information about the problem. Unaware of the theory, this is just what one of your authors began to do at De Montfort University when we started to drop in to lecture slots. Rather than saying that you can use X, Y, Z database for research on A, we talk through the stages that are involved in researching the assignment on a specific module, starting with keywords and resources, and demonstrating the results learners might expect to find.

This approach can be incredibly powerful: students listen actively because they think they are getting a key to the assignment (although in practice the same information has already been provided at induction and in guides or handbooks). It makes the content much more focused than at induction or in other information skills teaching sessions. It also applies the abstract knowledge of library and information professionals to subject and disciplinary contexts so as a teacher you can talk from a position of knowledge rather than trying to fit in with other patterns of work.

Encourage and build on early success

You can maintain interest and motivation by allowing learners to find ways to demonstrate their competence and avoid activities that will demonstrate their incompetence or lack of knowledge (Nicholls, 1984). This does not mean that you should over-simplify the content, but it does mean that you should not include elements that might be problematic and distract from your key objectives when giving a training session. A good example of this would be requiring a specific technical competence (like producing formatted bibliographies on Endnote) that is not essential to meeting the learning outcomes of an introductory session on searching databases.

Stipek (2002) suggests that learners will often respond to the challenge of the puzzle but that building in difficult barriers at an early stage will encourage disillusionment. Nothing will be as discouraging as failure, and some learners come with predefined expectations that they will fail. In planning you need to separate out activities that might be technically difficult from those that are intellectually challenging. Then consider whether you are aiming to train your learners to do tasks or teach them to think differently or accumulate new knowledge. Design your session accordingly.

The technique called scaffolding is useful in this context. Start simply but integrate ways of making the content more challenging and the work more independent as learners develop more confidence. For example, if giving training in searching databases, start a session with a tour around a website and finish it by giving examples of advanced searching techniques, reinforcing the content through plenty of practice.

Each time, think about setting a task to take the learner into what Vygotsky (1978) described as the 'zone of proximal development'. Learning can happen incrementally and the learners are encouraged by evidence of their growing capability. If you work with a very diverse group of learners you may need to set differential targets depending on your students' speed of work, ability or existing knowledge levels.

Provide feedback

Feedback is very important to learners. Build in opportunities to encourage, praise and provide developmental feedback. If you are not directly involved in formal assessment, build in some feedback to learners within your session. To continue with our database searching example, you might use the approach that one student uses to illustrate how you can search, and then to show how the search can be improved. At all times consider very carefully the language that you use, and avoid destructive criticism in favour of positive encouragement. As you become more comfortable with the processes try to encourage all types of feedback, from peers and externals as well as the teacher, and build these opportunities into your session design. If you are involved in any formal assessment, ensure that you include strategies for improvement alongside any criticism.

Online learning environments offer excellent opportunities for feedback, since as a teacher much of the interaction is captured through discussion or written responses. We will discuss this further in a later chapter.

Organize your material logically and make examples relevant and interesting

We will look at course design in Chapter 5 but you should reflect on how to make your material interesting, relevant and useful. Often we have to cover a lot of administrative detail (like how to log-on to a database) as well as skills development and it is easy to get bogged down. Think about how you will make information manageable and the tasks progressive. For example, if you are producing a workbook think about how you will close each section of content, and how the sections will link together.

In our experience we are often tempted to try and cover huge amounts of material in short sessions. This can result in overwhelming learners with content, but not giving them any meaning.

Another potential pitfall is using old or irrelevant material. Examples should be culturally relevant (so don't talk about a particular TV programme if your learners won't have seen it) and, if you work with younger people, remember that talking about something that happened five years ago will only make you seem out of touch. At the same time, don't try to be too trendy unless you can guarantee that your learners will relate to the examples, and that you won't look foolish.

Be ruthless with your content. The IT and information experience of our learners is changing every year, and it is dangerous to assume that what worked well one year will work again the next.

Remember as well that there is no model content or perfect course; any outlines we offer are for guidance only. What you teach should be your choice. You need to think about the needs of your learners, your facilities and the way that you prefer to do things as a teacher. When your authors teach, one of us is academic and theoretical, the other more practical. Both approaches are acceptable.

Assess

Assessment can be a powerful motivating factor but it can be over-emphasized. There are also significant cultural differences in attitudes to assessment, and you need to be sensitive to these as well. The main impact of assessment is that it increases the need, rather than the desire, to learn and this is often manifested as surface rather than deep learning. In an extensive study Isroff and del Soldato (1998) found that receiving bad marks motivated 42% of students but bad marks had no effect on 34% of the group. In our context, assessment is more powerful as a feedback mechanism, particularly within the context of a learning and teaching event. These issues are explored in more detail in Chapter 7.

Use the group

This is especially true with adult learners who bring a diverse mix of experiences and motivations to the learning experience. You can engage your students by setting activities and seeking input from group members. If the learners feel they are involved then they are likely to become more engaged and thus more motivated. This is not suggesting that you need not intervene: too low a profile can lead the learners to question why they should attend the learning event at all. A simple way of involving learners is to ask them to choose their break time or, if you are showing people how to use a database, get one of the learners to provide the examples or do the typing. The latter approach in particular can be an excellent way of engaging less interested students, since their focus of attention becomes their classmate who has been singled out.

Respond to the group

This links to an earlier point about over-preparing. Watch and listen to your group, rather than insisting on covering all the material you had planned to teach. If some examples do not work, just move on. There can be many reasons for this: the time of day, what else has happened to learners that day, personalities in the group and so on.

Try to be flexible, both in structure and style. When you are running a session, do not be afraid to hurry over parts that do not work with your particular class. Think about what practical work you will do and remember you can modify it depending on what feedback you get from the group. You will also find that using different language and presentation styles according to the sort of group you are working with can increase your influence over the students.

Most authors suggest that concentration levels flag after 20 minutes. Dividing any session up into 20-minute blocks of time can reduce the opportunity for boredom to creep in, as well as help you to structure and signpost your session.

Respond to learner diversity. Reflect on whether you have adopted learning and teaching strategies that are sensitive to the cultures and range of learning styles represented within your group, and your own timing. If it is an induction session, the group will often be less confident than if you are running a session for a community of people who already know each other.

Be careful not to demotivate

Remember that as a teacher you can demotivate learners through your behaviour, attitude and language. Don't:

- Be negative. Many people are far more likely to remember critical comments than positive ones.
- Give people unnecessary information. If you say too much, the message can be lost in the accompanying detail.
- Make inappropriate comments, such as making unfunny or unsuitable jokes, being too personal, or seeming too critical of your organization.
- Be late or overrun. Finishing earlier is a milder crime than finishing too late. It can be very difficult to get timing perfect. Sometimes you will find that the same material lasts different amounts of time depending on the group of learners you are with. At early stages, it is easy to overprepare. If this is the case, practice beforehand, and remember to allow for settling in, packing up and tea break time.

- Appear as if you do not care, or are defensive.
- Be too quiet.
- Lose control. Often as library and information professionals we work one-to-one with individuals and are supportive and tolerant. As a teacher you need to identify and maintain boundaries of how much support and advice you can give and what kinds of behaviour you will tolerate.

Very few of us are natural charismatic teachers: all of us can be effective ones.

Manage crises

Despite everything you can do, things can go wrong. Sometimes there may be conflicting personalities in the group, which lead to tensions that become manifest when trying to teach the students. This can be apparent both in face-to-face teaching environments, when the atmosphere seems unsettled, and online when online discussion or interaction does not work. As a teacher, you must be pragmatic and carry on. Remember that immediate reactions to content may not be identical to the lasting ones. Think about whether you have dismissed a session or course or teacher as worthless at the time only to realize later how valuable, interesting or useful the content of that teaching actually was.

Case study 3   Invisible students? Motivating e-learners

Freddie is running an online course for a group of learners all over the world. He is using a fairly standard software package – in this case conferencing software – and all the people on the course have been given advice and information on how to install the program on their own computers. There is also a supporting website with links to online resources and reading lists.

Anyone wishing to do this course has had to register and pay a fee and Freddie expects that most of the participants will be motivated because they have had to choose to do the course. The theme of the course is advanced information retrieval and management for library and information services staff, and Freddie is expecting an information and IT-literate community.

Freddie thought very carefully about design before building his course. He has produced a detailed teaching schedule, organized the distribution of materials well in advance and created virtual spaces for the learners to interact as well as a website with much of the material available online. Group work and discussion are important elements of the programme, because he expects that the learners will be able to find out a lot from each other.

The course has a few hiccups at the start. For no particular reason a lot of those registered on the course don't seem to be there at the beginning and a fair number still haven't contributed to any online discussions after the end of the second week.

Freddie is able to monitor attendance through the management options on the software. As the low participation rate continues he notices that there seem to be four distinct groups among his learners.

The first group is exceptionally enthusiastic. They are logging on frequently, posting lots of messages and truly engaging in the course and its material. Freddie finds their level of contribution almost alarming and dubs them the 'Netheads'. There is a second group who are participating but only by doing the minimum required. They are doing just enough to keep up with the course, so Freddie starts to call them the 'Minimalists'.

The other two groups are more worrying. The third group is the 'Silent minority'. They are logging on to the service but not posting any messages. They might be reading the content but have not been submitting any work. The final group is the 'Disappeared', who registered but have not logged on to the system.

Freddie is not sure what to do next. The course has an optional, credit-bearing assessment, which is a mixture of group and individual work. Freddie is not sure about how many people are actually participating on the course, and of these how many are likely to submit work for assessment. This uncertainty means that Freddie is undecided about how to organize participants for the group work part of the assessment, which in turn has an impact on the development of the rest of the course.

Questions

1. Do you recognize this typology from your own experience of working with groups of learners?
2. What can Freddie do next?

Discussion

Highly motivated and naturally enthusiastic groups of learners exist on film rather more often than they do in real life and although Freddie might expect a group of experienced professionals to get actively involved in a course like this, sometimes the rest of life gets in the way.

We don't really know that much about how Freddie has designed his course and what his expectations are as a tutor. There are several issues it might be helpful to know more about.

First of all, how aware if Freddie of the low completion rate in online and distance learning courses? We don't wish to appear negative, but it is a good idea to factor this in at the start. Completion rates will often fall below 50% in this mode of study, so has Freddie been a little over-optimistic in his course planning? The kind of people who choose to learn online at a distance have often made a conscious decision to study this way because they are do busy to take a traditional course. In turn this can mean that they find it difficult to make the space and time to participate even in this mode of learning.

Secondly, how did Freddie organize course induction and welcome activities? E-learners need to be welcomed into the new learning environment in just the same way as people starting more conventional courses. Indeed, sometimes people can take even longer to get started in an online environment than they did in the more traditional classroom and they can get disheartened more quickly. Reflect on your own experience of education and training: many of you will have stayed on a course or attended a specific class because you wanted to see the other students. This system of peer support is often slower to get started in online environments, although by the close of the course it will often be at least as strong.

Thirdly, how is Freddie building group identity and valuing individual contributions? It might be better to divide the learners into small groups and set individual tasks within the groups. This will speed up the establishment of cohort identity and perhaps start to foster the peer support and collaboration he wishes to achieve.

Fourthly, Freddie is monitoring attendance, but has he included any attendance requirement in the course? Though this may seem old-fashioned, it can be helpful to set rules for attendance and participation, so you can at least separate out who is attending and who isn't, and perhaps help students formally decide whether they wish to stay in or drop out.

Fifthly, Freddie has identified the Netheads and the Minimalists as two different groups. Could the Netheads be intimidating to the Minimalists (albeit unintentionally)? How clearly has Freddie established the netiquette between his groups of learners?

Finally, does Freddie need to think a bit about his role as an e-tutor or e-moderator? How actively is he leading the course?

Case study 4   Getting into the culture in further education

Alex works in the Learning Resources Centre (LRC) in a college of further education that serves a largely urban and industrial community. The LRC merges library, IT, media and learning support services in a mixture of purpose-built and former classroom accommodation across the college, which specializes in vocational and technical subjects, with students taking a range of courses from basic skills to foundation degrees.

Sometimes the LRC can seem more like a social area than a library and when she first started Alex sometimes found the gangs of students hanging around the building a little intimidating. Behaviour from some groups could be challenging and Alex found her assertiveness skills, developed from funding her studies by doing bar work, very useful on several occasions. Alex has had a mixed experience of doing information skills sessions. Sometimes students seem to join in and do what they have been asked to complete, at other times groups get easily distracted and try to mess around. Some of her academic colleagues could also be heard muttering darkly about what had happened in classes they had run, so Alex was pretty sure that the LRC staff were not treated any worse than teaching staff, but nevertheless it did not always feel like an ideal teaching environment.

Alex was in two minds when Mike Bailey, a business studies lecturer, asked if she would run an information skills session for some of his Advanced GNVQ business students. After some consideration Alex agreed to run a two-hour workshop the content of which would be linked to some coursework students would be doing that term.

The idea behind the class was that the students needed to be able to research a company and a market, looking at how the business and marketing environment influences its operation and management. The students had already attended an LRC library induction, so the aim of the session was for the students to use and evaluate material from a range of sources rather than orienting themselves around the LRC. The week before her session Alex sat in on a class, just to introduce herself and to find out a bit more about the students. To her dismay they just seemed like a big group of rather naughty boys. Two students at the back spent a lot of their class time reading the sports sections of tabloid papers rather than concentrating on any academic work, which did not augur well for the LRC-based class.

Question

1.   What would you do if you were Alex?

Discussion

When it came to it, Alex and her class had a really enjoyable and useful information skills session. Alex realized that it would probably be best to concentrate on active learning approaches and to try to find a topic that would harness her students' imagination and energy.

After sitting in on the class the previous week, Alex wondered what might be a good starting point for the class. She knew that this group consisted entirely of male students (this was quite unusual) and that as well as the two newspaper readers nearly all the students were arrayed in some form of sportswear, with football accessories being particularly popular.

Alex thought long and hard about what to do and decided that she would get them to search for information on a football club and to introduce a competitive element into the class to motivate them a bit more. When the day came, she introduced the idea to the class. This is what she told them:

- Work in groups of four.
- Choose a football club.
- Find out what you can about the club as a business and how the external business and marketing environment is influencing it.
- Present your findings to the rest of the class.
- The rest of the class will award you marks for presentation, the search strategies you have adopted and the level of information you find.
- The winning group gets a prize (of chocolate, which Alex had purchased for the occasion).

This had taken Alex a while to plan and prepare. She had to make sure that the teaching space was suitable, that the class had access to the right range of sources and that pens and flipchart paper or OHPs were available. She had to work out her timings carefully, too, in particular thinking about how much she should say at the beginning as an introduction and how much she could leave for the students to find out for themselves. She had also produced an assessment sheet with guidelines for marking the presentations so that this part of the session could be standardized.

The session worked very successfully. Alex had managed to energize the students by picking a topic that they were interested in, adding in a bit of competition and making the learning active. The workshop time passed by quickly and students found the competitive element an incentive to do their best.

Feedback from Mike Bailey the next week was pretty positive too – it was clear that the students had genuinely enjoyed the session and Mike and Alex both hoped it would make a difference to their study.

4 Auditing: finding out what your learners need

It is not uncommon for teachers to spend considerable amounts of time preparing courses or materials which become useless on contact with the learners. This may be because of environmental factors like computer failure or a group that contains difficult personalities, but often it is because the teacher has not audited learner needs and expectations. Many of us can recall having had these difficulties when attending short courses or conferences – the content did not match expectations or our experiences. We will discuss setting and clarifying learning outcomes in Chapter 5, but there is a stage before this where content and delivery are shaped by what you know about your learners.

The process of finding out what your learners need and expect from the session is called auditing. It is rarely discussed in most of the texts on how to teach, perhaps because teachers or university lecturers know what content to cover and often have several weeks or months for delivery. Even texts on the design of training (as opposed to teaching) rarely mention auditing. Yet most teachers and trainers use their sessions to audit understanding and modify or develop content and delivery as the course progresses. Since library and information professionals are more often working in a 'one-shot' teaching environment – you see your learners once for a single session – it becomes more important to assess learner needs at the beginning to maximize the value that can be drawn from the event.

Auditing is possibly the hardest element in the learning and teaching process for library and information professionals. You will find that learner knowledge and experience levels vary widely even among individuals with very similar backgrounds. It is often necessary to challenge preconceptions and expectations about the role of libraries, of the informational value of the internet or the validity of library or information service mediated information and about the scope and level at which you can teach and train other people. At the same time we have little control over the timing and organization of our sessions, since to a large extent we are dependent on other people – teachers, managers, and so on – to gain access to our learners.

This episodic nature of teaching means that as teachers we focus on preparing content rather than meeting our learners and working out how we can reach them most effectively. After all, if you teach only occasionally, it can be challenging enough to ensure that the content is suitable, without adding in other risks, variables and uncertainties.

This chapter has a more practical orientation than the others you have read so far in this book. This is simply because there is very little research and theory about auditing learning, with a notable exception being the very approachable book by Milne and Noone (1996). We will discuss more systematic approaches like training needs analysis but they have a limited application in most instances.

What is auditing?

The purpose of auditing is to assess the following in your learners:

- *Motivation and expectations* How much do you understand about why your learners are participating in this event and what do you know about what they wish to achieve? You should attempt to fulfil expressed and implicit needs and expectations and recognize them in the learning outcomes that you set – see Chapter 5 for more discussion of this.
- *The range of learning styles present in your group of learners* For example, teaching based around abstract theory will not work with activist or pragmatist learners. You need to change your approach, even if you

cover very similar content. For example, you can use different approaches to running sessions with undergraduates, postgraduates and part-time students depending on the learners and their academic culture even if the sources covered are very similar. See the discussion of Kolb in Chapter 2.

- *Diversity* Basing a session around a current popular national television programme would not be very successful if you are working with international students, or using examples that are dated or culturally or socially inappropriate.
- *Levels of experience and expertise* You need to know where to pitch your content. It would be pointless and disheartening for all concerned to explain how to access and use the controlled vocabulary in a database only to discover that few of your learners had ever used a computer with a mouse. Equally, remember that just because people have little experience or expertise in one area, it does not mean that they will not understand complex ideas. You just need to know where to start.

Once you have this information you can be more confident in planning and designing your learning and teaching event. Sometimes the audit process can be very straightforward, but at other times you will still find that you are starting a teaching session with very little information about your learners, and your auditing has to be embedded within delivery and particularly the activities that you set.

Auditing is based on the principle that you can make learning more effective if it appears to meet needs and expectations, and that the content is suitable for your learners. It is a learner-centred, rather than teacher-led, approach to the design of learning, since its purpose is for the teacher to understand more about the learner. At one level auditing is to do with understanding the values and emotions of your learners. Often we find that our learners either have negative expectations of the 'library' or of themselves, and much of our teaching is based around finding ways to get our learners both to value themselves more highly and to realize the importance of information skills.

Auditing in practice

Thus auditing is the process of finding out about your learners and using that information in your teaching. Some of the approaches you can adopt are discussed below.

Asking the learners

The most straightforward way of auditing existing knowledge, experience and expectations is by asking the learners about them directly at the beginning of your learning and teaching event. You can use the responses to your questions to confirm that you have prepared appropriately and you are going to start at the right level and cover the right kind of content.

The easiest way to do this is by asking individual, direct questions. In a face-to-face environment you might do this by speaking to your learners individually as they arrive. If you are running a longer session or series of sessions you will find that you can easily integrate this auditing process into the welcome, introductions and warm-up exercises at the beginning of the day.

Remember though that people may not always assess their capabilities accurately. It can be more useful to ask experience-based questions like 'Can you tell me which search engine you use?' or 'What sorts of information you have found more difficult to trace?' than 'How do you rate your effectiveness at searching the internet?' You can further develop this approach through using critical incidents – asking people to recall something important to them or to talk through a 'What happens next' scenario. You should consider as well whether the feedback you receive from your learners tallies with your observation of them, and use both sources in making any judgements.

Auditing can be a very effective introduction to a session. For example, when working with mature learners or postgraduate students you encounter very diverse groups, which often contain some people who cannot understand why they need to be 'shown around the library again'. When meeting your learners, just asking them if they have used this library before, and even how long it is since they used any library, can make a very effective start to the session. Adult learners particularly like to be acknowledged as individuals, and if you show you are interested in them as people it can be a way of reducing their resistance to what may not have seemed a useful way of spending their time. You will also gauge their levels of experience and get some feedback about particular concerns.

If you are running a course of several sessions remember that you will need to continue to audit – to check knowledge and understanding – as the content becomes more complex or as new ideas are introduced. It can be easier to see this latter process as assessment and we will discuss approaches to doing this in Chapter 7.

Designing the session based on learner feedback

Rather than using your questions as a way of checking that your preparation was appropriate you can use the audit as the start of the creative enquiry that forms the heart of the session. This can be particularly effective in informal situations.

The teaching session is more like an interactive reference interview, with the teacher asking questions and then shaping the whole of the learning experience in response to feedback from the learners. This is a freeform approach, and can be incredibly enriching and fulfilling for both teachers and learners. The content of the teaching is built around learners' needs and what they bring to the session. As a teacher you shape the learning experience actively and creatively to produce a dialogue or tutorial tailored to the learners.

However, use this approach with caution. Many learners want to be told what to do. They expect the teacher to set the agenda and are comforted by structure and evidence of advance preparation. Learners want the teacher to be in control and have traditional and passive expectations of your role. They see this informal, dialogue-based question-and-answer mode of teaching only as evidence that the teacher is under-prepared and is trying to work our how little he or she needs to do to run the course.

In practice, it is probably best to adopt this creative approach when you are a confident teacher and feel sufficiently in control of your material.

You might also prefer to use this method when working with small groups of adult learners when it is probably most effective. Remember that you should always be aware that the freeform approach is an option, and do not feel that you should never digress from your planned content: if you reflect on your own experiences as a learner you might find that diversions were often the most memorable part of lessons.

Interviewing

Another option is to interview the people you will be training before your session takes place. Contact your learners individually (either face-to-face, by telephone or by e-mail) and interview them. You might structure your discussion around the purpose of the session and the kind of content they might like to cover, especially if there are particular areas they would be interested in investigating. If you are running informal training courses for professionals within your organization this is a powerful and very effective approach. It can be especially useful if you want to get access to influential people – you offer customized training, and you can come prepared.

Carrying out self-assessment

A more systematic (and time-consuming) approach to auditing is through using some form of self-assessment. You can do this before the learning event or at the beginning of the session. You then find out what your learners know already, their expectations and some information about them.

In order to do this, you can use a number of different approaches. In more formal teaching and training environments, especially at the beginning of a course (several hours or sessions), it can be easiest to audit learner needs by distributing a pre-course activity. This is particularly effective if you are using e-learning, since the activity can also serve as an induction to the technology, netiquette, and so on before the main delivery starts but it can be equally effective in a face-to-face induction where participants have been asked to prepare something in advance.

In an online environment you might ask people to introduce themselves and say what they want from the course, or require them to answer a specific question. You can use this audit activity to find out more about the learners, without causing lots of difficulties about missed content for any late starters.

A second approach is using a questionnaire. This can be particularly useful if you are very concerned with evaluating the effectiveness of your training, or gathering other data about your target population. You need to build in a considerable amount of time for this approach, however, since you should design and pilot the questionnaire before distributing it, and then allow more time for responses and your analysis. You will also need to think carefully about the kind of questions you will ask and think about how you will use the information that you acquire.

The questionnaire can be distributed to participants before the teaching and learning event or handed out at the beginning of the session. The timing will have some effect on the kind of information you collect and how you might use it.

A pre-session questionnaire can give you scope for quite a lot of data collection. You should reflect on whether you want to use it to test knowledge, needs, expectations or experience levels. Try to make it as simple as possible. Remember, you have not yet told your learners what the session will contain, so you are asking for responses from people who may not have been provided with very much background.

Think therefore of what kinds of questions might be straightforward to answer. Rather than asking about people's experience of libraries, which can be very subjective, it will be easier to survey IT skills or ask about the kinds of information most often required.

Remember as well that by completing a questionnaire your learners will have been provided with the opportunity to reflect on the learning event ahead, and thus to focus on their needs and expectations and to communicate them with the teacher. It can therefore serve three quite different objectives. First of all it can provide an opportunity for learners to reflect on their needs and wants and get ready to learn. Secondly, you can establish trust with the learners by seeming concerned about them. Finally, you are gathering information to use in designing your session.

You may even find that the feedback from the questionnaire gives your learners the opportunity to choose or prioritize what they do in their formal information skills sessions. If you are using an online tutorial, questionnaire results might suggest that your learners start at level one or level two. If you are running workshops, you might be able to offer more choice to accommodate the diversity of your learner needs.

If you issue a questionnaire at the beginning of the session you have rather less sophisticated outcomes. At first you will have a 'quick and dirty' source of information (unanalysed data) but you will also have built some links with your learners, and you might still be able to use the data constructively. For example, one of the authors started a series of lectures on the information society and information retrieval by getting students to complete a questionnaire on the way that they used the internet. Responses were collected, scanned for any useful information as the session began and later analysed and fed back to the learners in the next lecture to demonstrate how their experience and use of the internet compared with published research.

There is a third option – to use a multiple-choice questionnaire with some pre-designed feedback at the beginning of a session. It is less spontaneous as an approach and you will need to give a lot of thought to your responses, but there may be some merit in testing this approach.

Discussing with third party

In many situations it is not the learners who create their own learning opportunity. In formal educational and workplace environments, the decision to have information skills training is often taken by the learners' tutor or manager.

This means that rather than building the content of a session around the expressed needs of your group of learners, you are often fitting in to requirements expressed by a third party, who is usually in a position of some authority. In an educational context a tutor might ask for an information skills session based around a specific assignment or project, or in a workplace a manager might request that all staff in one area be trained to use certain databases effectively.

The manager or tutor will be able to supply you with quite a lot of information about who your learners are and what they need to gain from your session. You may need to negotiate timings and structure of the session. For example, tutors often request 'library sessions' without being any more specific. If you can find ways of contextualizing your information skills session, you can make the session more focused and thus more effective for all concerned. This may require some careful questioning of the manager or tutor, but can help to establish a productive professional relationship in the future.

Carrying out a training needs analysis

A much more systematic and comprehensive approach can be found in training needs analysis (TNA). This is based on matching individual learning needs to organizational requirements or goals; rather than having a goal of personal development (as in much adult education) or successful academic achievement (in formal educational environments), its focus is on maximizing performance for corporate objectives.

The focus of training needs analysis is therefore on the whole organization, and will mean that a wider array of information is used in planning the teaching and learning opportunity and certainly in producing a rationale for the activity. This will include business and operational plans as well as information about individual members of staff. Training needs analysis is often future-facing, linked to strategic organizational objectives, with the training programme being used as a catalyst for change.

Boydell and Leary (1996) offer a detailed discussion of training needs analysis and emphasize its scale, stressing that it requires process, relationship and content management skills. The best starting point for anyone wishing to conduct a training needs analysis is Williamson's (1993) training guide, which is clear and comprehensive.

In an information skills context this approach clearly has some potential, particularly if there are moves towards end-user access to specialist resources. In this scenario, TNA would be useful to identify user training and support requirements and also the new mediation skills required from LIS staff. Donnelly and Craddock (2002) provide a very interesting account of an information literacy programme at Unilever.

Triangulation of evidence

Triangulation is an important concept when gathering data. It is the process of verifying the accuracy of what you have found by finding some more evidence to create another reference point. For example, you might ask your learners what they know and then test them. As well as all the cultural and motivational dimensions we have already explored, remember that most research finds that people overrate their effectiveness in information search and retrieval. So if you ask a group of learners if they are good at searching the internet, you might find that in practice they are much less sophisticated searchers than they claim to be.

Equally, remember that skill levels are changing constantly. It is easy to assume that the kind of content you used with a group once will work the next time you run the same sort of session or course. This can be a dangerous assumption. Often you will find that your learners' skills and competences will be different each time you teach the session, so you will need to shift the emphasis of your teaching.

What happens if you do not audit?

If you ignore this audit stage when preparing your learning and teaching event there are several risks. You may create demotivated and alienated learners who have disengaged from a session that appears to offer them nothing. Or you might just bore your learners by making them repeat learning they have already achieved. What is more stressful is if you cause confusion by requiring your learners to process something that requires prior knowledge or experience or is expressed in a way that they cannot understand. It is unacceptable to make the learners withdraw from the learning experience by forcing them into actions or activities that are inappropriate, for example insisting on learners giving individual oral feedback to the whole group when their language skills are poor. The impact of a failure to audit will often be a failure to learn, either through lack of comprehension or withdrawal.

Finally, remember that auditing is not an end in itself. You can rarely find out so much that every part of your teaching matches all your learners' needs exactly, nor should you. If you want to develop learning skills remember that it can be useful to get people to explore different learning and teaching techniques and approaches, but start at least from a position of understanding something about your learners. Doing preparatory work about the needs of your learners through auditing complements the other elements of your teaching in order to make it a satisfactory experience for all.

Case study 5   Auditing local historians

Linda has been working as the local studies librarian for a public library authority for several years. She spends a large proportion of her time helping members of the public research their family history. She found that she needed to give a lot of directive support to people, and a lot of the time she found she was going through the same sources time and again with different people, but often in an unstructured and fairly haphazard way.

Linda and her manager decided that as a trial it might be a good idea to run a workshop on how to research your family history, with the objective of promoting the local studies collection and developing more independence among its users. There was even the option of working with the local adult education centre to turn this into a certificated course if this worked out well.

A little to Linda's surprise the pilot workshop booked up fairly quickly with 12 people – the maximum she was hoping for. Linda spent a lot of time getting her room ready, preparing her handouts and working on a script of what she would say. Her plan was to give a talk and introduction at the beginning and then people would have the chance to use sources, printed and online, following instructions developed from information guides already available.

On the day itself Linda was pleased that most of the workshop attendees turned up early but was rather dismayed to see that the group ranged from two young teenagers to some businesslike-looking retired people. Somehow she hadn't imagined that her first group would be quite so diverse!

She started the session as planned but things started to go wrong when it became apparent that two of the participants had very specific agendas.

Don, a man of indeterminate age, had very definite opinions, which he was keen to voice. He interrupted repeatedly and kept contradicting Linda. Sally was the second challenge, since it was quickly obvious that she had a personal problem about adoption. Linda wasn't quite sure exactly what it was and felt unconfident about how to handle it whatever happened.

The whole session unravelled even further when it came to the practical element. Linda realized that the 11 people in the class were even more diverse than she had initially expected. They had very mixed ability, ranging from expert amateur local historians (who just wanted some specialist advice) to complete novices (who needed to have everything explained). More troubling to Linda was someone who seemed to have special educational needs – certainly he seemed to have problems with reading and understanding anything Linda said, and was not able to write. The two teenagers who had come were actually researching local rather than family history for some coursework but their teacher had thought that there wouldn't be much difference in what would be covered. In addition one of the novices was completely technophobic and refused to use a computer. Don continued to contradict and undermine Linda and the atmosphere became tense between him and the other participants. Sally kept pressing Linda for information about adoption records and how much could be traced.

Linda felt very torn – who should she help first and how? The result seemed to be that the experts got bored and frustrated as Linda tried to get the novices started before helping them with their enquiries; the teenagers got distracted and started messing around on the internet. Meanwhile the technophobe looked about ready to burst into tears and Don got nastier.

Eventually the two hours planned for the course had elapsed and Linda was able to wind up the session. Rather to her surprise the feedback wasn't as bad as she was dreading, with some very nice comments from a couple of participants about how valuable the session had been. Linda's personal appraisal was rather less enthusiastic. She had not enjoyed this experience at all, and it confirmed her secret fear that she wasn't really cut out for teaching and training. The next day she found out that the local adult education centre was very keen to pursue the option of a certificated course, so she would need to continue to run her workshop. Linda sighed and started to think about what she could do next.

Questions

1. What did Linda do right?
2. Could she have stopped things going quite so wrong?

Discussion

You can often be your own worst critic and events like Linda's workshop can be very traumatic. It is a truism but often things can only get better. Our lack of experience in working with learners in these formal course environments can often mean that we don't have the same kind of flexibility and level of confidence possessed by more experienced teachers. Sometimes circumstances conspire to bring you what we flippantly describe as 'a group from hell', and you just need to survive these sessions. Even so, do not underestimate the value of well-prepared content. Some of the learners would have found the talk, the handouts and the opportunity for some structured learning more than sufficient: you do not need to be at every learner's side. Perhaps Linda might have used some auditing techniques to standardize expectations and this might have made the course easier. These are some of her alternatives.

First of all, in order to book a place on the course potential participants could be required to fill in a short form. This would be a good way of finding out about prior knowledge and experience, and might alert Linda that there was someone with additional needs likely to attend so she could be prepared.

Secondly, Linda could think about running different kinds of courses: one for beginners and one for experienced researchers. She would have to define what she meant by experienced and beginner to try to ensure that only suitable people attended whichever course, and still be prepared for some misunderstanding, but it might reduce the extremes in experience she encountered. She could think about what learners might require before attending a course, for example specifying that even for the beginners course participants should be able to use the internet.

Another option would be for Linda to think about alternative delivery methods, and perhaps look at developing her handouts into a series of worksheets with activities, which could be used by different ability groups, even within the same workshop.

Linda might have spent a bit longer with the introductions and then for the practical work asked the learners to work together in groups of two or three. That would mean that the session became less unwieldy (five groups rather than 11 individuals) and there would be scope for some peer tutoring and peer support.

Linda might also consider whether the group size was too big and that next time she needs to run a class for a group no larger than eight.

People like Don and Sally can be very distracting to teachers and to fellow students. Linda did her best not to let them divert the class, and she tried her assertiveness techniques to quieten Don. She should remember that she could always ask him to leave if he is causing offence.

Finally, Linda might think about using team teaching approaches by asking a colleague to help her out: that reduces the number of learners to the teacher and increases the amount of personal support available.

Case study 6   Auditing in the workplace

One of the biggest changes facing many workplace libraries is the shift from mediated services and enquiry handling to direct end-user access to resources. Thus the role of the librarian or information professional has shifted from being the person who finds the information (the gopher) to being the person who acquires and manages resources and supports others in their use. In many information-intensive organizations, like government libraries, management consultancies or law firms, this can be a challenge since it requires a redefinition of roles and professional boundaries and constant justification of the need to have a workplace library or information service, rather than purely disintermediated access to resources.

The case for information skills becomes a strategic issue for the information service. Not only must it ensure that its resources provide value for money but the contribution played by information professionals in managing and supporting those services must also be recognized. In some organizations an information skills support strategy has been developed to achieve exactly these objectives – although rarely under that name.

Nila was the manager of an information service in a City-based law firm. As in most legal organizations, information was the life-blood of professional practice. Lawyers needed extensive access to sources, ranging from case law and legislation to company information when dealing with corporate clients.

The majority of legal information resources were available through the corporate intranet and the law library had a greater virtual presence than a physical one. Even most of the practitioner guides were published on the web or on networked CD-ROM. Nila had worked for this law firm for several years and still couldn't get over the transition she had seen sweeping through the organization. When she started there as a humble temporary assistant, trainee solicitors used to be sent to the library to find out all sorts of information. They were often quite reluctant to use a PC, even though they were generally very confident individuals. Very few of the partners expressed any interest in online information and a lot more made their secretaries check and respond to any e-mail messages that colleagues had the temerity to send them. What a culture change! OK, well perhaps one of the senior partners still didn't use a computer himself, but he was still an e-enthusiast in rhetoric if not reality. Nila thought he still made his secretary do this just because that was the way he was most comfortable working. Certainly he was very good at applying his keen legal intelligence to income generation and the management of the firm, so it was hard to condemn him for avoiding what could be a rather overwhelming e-mail traffic at busy times.

But Nila had a couple of concerns nagging away inside her. From some of the enquiries she received she was not entirely convinced that the trainee solicitors (the recent graduates) were as conversant with the legal resources available as they might be. Secondly, she wasn't sure that people were using the most appropriate resources. Her usage statistics indicated that a couple of online services were used heavily, but others were not being used as much as she would have predicted. Nila considered what to do next. If she wanted to arrange some training and awareness-raising, what would she need to do?

Questions

1. What advice would you give to Nila?
2. What barriers might she encounter and how would she overcome them?

Discussion

Probably the first issue for Nila is to investigate the scope of the potential training needs. She does not need to establish a large-scale programme if those needs could be met just as effectively through improved induction processes and increased awareness of resources. It might be that the two most popular databases meet her users' needs so well that, even though alternatives exist, the costs of learning another interface and wasting time searching yet another database are greater than the information benefit obtained. Perhaps then she needs to review her acquisitions policies and service development plans.

Nila has a number of options in how she could investigate training needs. She already has some hard data in the form of usage statistics, but this is open to interpretation as we have already pointed out. She could conduct a systematic training needs analysis, but has she really got the time and resources and the goodwill to do this in an organization dedicated to external income generation?

We would suggest that she might use quite a low-key approach to developing her training programme, but that she is proactive in developing her own skills. To start with, we strongly recommend that she attend a suitable training course. Previously she has been more expert at finding, managing and presenting information than acting as a facilitator and intermediary. Teaching and learning support skills are different from her usual area of expertise and it might help Nila to approach this work from a fresh perspective.

Next, we advise Nila to arrange some meetings with section managers to talk about the information and support needs of their units. In effect Nila will be conducting training needs analysis through interviewing key stakeholders, but of course she would also be able to use the information for general service development. And she might even use these meetings as an opportunity to do some one-to-one coaching, which can often be the most convincing case for increased input. After all, if the senior managers endorse your activities and support your mission, the path to success is much more clearly illuminated.

From these interviews we hope that Nila would be able to establish a set of priorities for action. If she finds that she should mainly focus on the trainee solicitors, she might need to consider whether she can find a way of embedding her training sessions into the firm's standard training programme, so it is timetabled and gets formal recognition.

Alternatively, she might find that she needs to work with a few key individuals in sections. These people might be professional support lawyers who do not work directly with clients but who co-ordinate information within their unit. These people do the highest volume of legal research and are also the key gatekeepers.

A third option would be to focus on running training sessions for a wider range of people. If this is the case she should liaise with Human Resources and see if participants can accrue some CPD credits either from attendance or completion of assessed work.

Of course auditing is only the starting point in developing her training role, but Nila has got quite a lot to get started with! This might not be easy for her. She will have to negotiate access to busy and important people for her interviews, convince them of the benefits of a new approach and change her own role. At the same time, what she is fundamentally trying to do is align her work and that of her department with organizational requirements as they themselves shift in response to internal and external drivers. In order to continue to be relevant and cost-effective, Nila needs to change with the times.

5 Planning a learning experience

In the previous three chapters we have focused on the needs, motivation and experience of learners. In this and the next two chapters we will be looking at how you can shape and focus a learning and teaching event through planning, delivery and assessment respectively.

Planning is critical to the teaching process. Good planning enables you to clarify what you wish to achieve and create the right kind of opportunities to enable this to happen. In this chapter we will explore a number of topics, including the preparation and use of aims, objectives and learning outcomes, planning content and structure, getting ready to deliver a session, some specific considerations for e-learning and reflections on the planning process. In our experience, effective planning is often the determining factor in successful teaching, and perhaps the easiest element you can improve and enhance whatever your working context.

Planning in context

Throughout this book we suggest that it is important for you to step back from delivering information skills teaching and facilitating learning to review what you are doing. In other words, you must adopt a reflective and critical perspective on the ways you teach and deliver your training. This professional model not only serves to make you more aware of your own inputs and how to modify and develop them, but it will also help you to empathize with learners. This approach will mirror your own professional practice in other areas of library and information work.

In a widely influential text, Ramsden (1992) describes the underlying goal of teaching as enabling learners to experience changes in understanding. Following this argument the purpose of planning is to address what might be described as the journalist's six Ws:

- *Who?* Who are our learners and what are their needs?
- *What?* What do they need to know and how is this decided?
- *When?* When (and for how long) will the learning event take place?
- *Where?* What is the location – physical or virtual? What equipment do I have? What is the size of the group and other questions related to the learning environment?
- *Why?* What expectations are there for the session and what will its outcomes be? Is there a link to assessment?
- *How?* What learning and teaching methods will I use? What activities will I plan? How can I assess that my objectives have been met?

When teaching information skills there are many positive outcomes from effective planning. At the most basic level, good planning will mean that all the materials and resources you need are ready, and you are clear about what you wish to do. Your clarity about the purpose of the sessions can also be communicated to the learners, and help build trust and understanding with them. Setting learning outcomes facilitates assessment and evaluation of the process.

On a personal level, planning helps you to think about your input into learning and teaching. Milne and Noone (1996) discuss the importance of identifying learning needs both through auditing and reflection. In their view reflection helps to identify different sets of needs (Milne and Noone, 1996, 31). These include:

- *Expressed needs of learners* Where the role of the teacher is to convert the learners' felt needs into expressed needs; Chapter 4 has already discussed this in terms of the auditing process, and we will look at writing aims and objectives in more detail in this chapter.

- *Teacher's needs* Where planning enables the teacher or learning facilitator to take control of the learning and teaching process; developing goals, priorities and sense of ownership of the learning process, feeling effective and thus increasing confidence.
- *Normative need* What learners should be taught based on the teacher's knowledge of the subject or assessment or external requirements.
- *Comparative needs* What the teacher thinks this group needs in relation to previous experience with similar groups, in library induction sessions for example.

In our view, this reflective process starts the planning cycle since focusing on needs will lead to the development of aims and objectives and thence to effective design for learning. In relatively few instances are we required to deliver an externally set curriculum, so we select our context. Depending on your personal approach you might think about these issues before you start planning a session or, if you have a more practical orientation, use an awareness of these needs as prompts through your preparation and planning.

The planning process

According to Ramsden, 'Decisions about which methods to use in order to teach and assess our students should be based on their effectiveness as a means of encouraging high quality learning outcomes, which by definition are concerned with subject content and the people who learn that content' (Ramsden, 1992, 125). Put more simply, everything derives from the aims, objectives and learning outcomes.

Perhaps the clearest, most relevant and action-oriented guide to the planning process for information skills teaching was produced in the EduLib portfolio (McNamara and Core, 1998, 85). Seven stages were identified:

- Specify the aims and outcomes for the session.
- Plan how to check that the learning outcomes have been attained – plan the assessment (whether or not you are actually going to carry out a formal assessment).

- Plan the learning activities to enable the attainment of specified learning outcomes.
- Plan the inputs, both presentations and resource-based materials to enable the attainment of specified learning outcomes.
- Sequence and timetable the session.
- Plan how to obtain feedback for the session.
- Lay out an appropriate learning environment.

Although this can seem a prescriptive approach this is not at all the case. Rather it is a framework you can apply with increasing amounts of freedom as your confidence as a teacher increases.

Aims, objectives and learning outcomes

The starting point of the process is the specification of aims, objectives and learning outcomes. See Figure 5.1. First of all, it will be helpful to define what we mean by aims, objectives and learning outcomes
If we look at these in terms of a driving lesson:

- The aim is for you to learn to drive a car.
- The objectives will be that you will learn and practise how to steer, change gear, manoeuvre, and so on.
- The learning outcome will be that by the end of the lesson(s) you will be able to pass a driving test and be recognized as a competent driver.

An *aim* encapsulates what you are trying to achieve with the learning event.

An *objective* shows how you are going to reach the aim.

The *learning outcome* is another, more learner-centred, way of defining the purpose of the teaching by describing what changes in understanding will have been achieved by the learners, after teaching has taken place.

Figure 5.1 Definition of aims, objectives and learning outcomes

You can also describe the same three elements in these simple questions:

- What do these learners need to know?
- How will we get there?
- How can I tell whether we have been successful?

The aims, objectives and learning outcomes can be set by the teacher, by the learners, or by both of you in what Milne and Noone describe as a 'learning alliance' (1996, 36). The way in which they are set will depend very much on the situation, your preferences as a teacher and the needs of the learners. In the previous chapters we have discussed in some detail the different approaches that you will adopt depending on the needs of your learners. The same principles apply when setting aims and objectives.

In our experience, when running formal courses our learners often expect the teacher or trainer to set the aims, objectives and learning outcomes. In this way the tutor defines the nature and boundary of the teaching and learning adventure. Equally, when you are working in an informal situation you might expect your learners to construct their own learning outcomes for themselves through the enquiry or tutorial process. As a tutor you discover them through the audit process and use this knowledge to construct meaning through the teaching and learning process. And there is of course a third way: times when tutor and learners work together to shape the preferred aims, objectives and learning outcomes. This happens most often when you are working with experienced learners who are working at one remove from their normal work – with professionals or managers using resources outside their normal sphere of experience, for example. These are often people who can see clear applications for their new knowledge but who do not share your formal language or abstract understanding.

These differing ways of setting aims, outcomes and learning objectives create subtly different ways of defining and assessing whether they actually work. In the teacher-centred model we focus on planning, describing the inputs and objectives. In the student-centred model we perhaps think more of outcomes and in particular the learning outcomes. In the middle path we merge the two together. No one way is more valid in absolute terms. It all depends on what you are trying to do and who your learners are.

Introducing aims, objectives and learning outcomes

Turning now to the more practical application of these ideas, we need to consider how to introduce goals into your learning event.

If as the teacher or facilitator you decide on the aims you must still explain them to the learners. Explaining the purpose and focus of the session clarifies what you are trying to achieve. It removes the sense of purposelessness that many of us must have felt in our own experiences as learners and more importantly creates a sense of mutual understanding and shared direction in the teaching session. This will mean you can engage the learners by getting them to accept what you want to do and setting targets, goals and assessment criteria for meeting those objectives. This serves to make your teaching intellectually coherent and fair to the learners; these are essential educational values.

In a formal teaching environment, the most orthodox way of presenting your learning goals is through an introduction at the beginning of your class. You may choose to do this by starting a lecture by saying what the intended learning outcomes will be or by putting statements of the same outcomes on handouts or slides.

If you want your learners to create their own aims, objectives and learning outcomes you must plan some time into an overall lesson or course design for this element and consider the effect this will have on the rest of your session. In the most informal environment you might do this through discussion with your learners about what they need. In a classroom this might form a discrete activity at the beginning of the session and the whole of the course content depends on this input. When you feel confident in your role as a teacher it can be enjoyable and effective. We would advise that you use this method when you have some experience, but do not be reluctant to experiment when you have the confidence and time.

In the learning alliance the onus is on the tutor to prepare material that can be contextualized to meet the needs of the student. A popular approach is to get your learners to write up their needs and wants at the beginning of the session or e-learning course and to review to what extent they have been met at the end. One way of doing this is by asking participants to complete Post-it™ notes about what their questions, problems or concerns are and then put them onto a flipchart. Another way to achieve the same goal is through open-ended discussion, perhaps introduced through group work – 'Perhaps you might like to talk in groups of two or three about what you would like to take away from the workshop' – or through online discussion.

You can choose how explicit you wish to make your aims, objectives and learning outcomes. In our universities in the UK they normally appear in course outlines, module handbooks and when introducing each session; this is our current orthodoxy. In other working environments it might be acceptable to make them more implicit or spend less time in making them explicit. You can and should choose how to do this, but remember much educational research suggests that if you make learners aware of the goals of the teaching, they are more likely to participate fully (Ramsden, 1992; Biggs, 2003). Nevertheless, just thinking and working out how your learners can assess how they will have met the learning outcomes from their learning and learning event can make the whole experience much more powerful and thought provoking than was first intended.

In terms of creating the whole learning and teaching experience, link your aims, objectives and learning outcomes to assessment. Try to think of assessment as a way of testing and validating the new knowledge and skills acquired by your learners. In earlier chapters we looked at theories of learning and motivation and in many of these some form of assessment – of practice, personal reflection and feedback – is critical to the success of the learning experience. We will discuss this idea in much more detail in Chapter 7.

It is always good practice to review the goals when you conclude the session. If you are running an interactive teaching session you can ask participants about the extent to which they feel the learning outcomes have been met, perhaps through reviewing statements they made at the beginning of the class in the example given above. In less participative environments you should review the learning outcomes through slides or handouts at the close of the session.

It is worth noting here that there are some criticisms of this approach. Sometimes it is argued that using aims, objectives and learning outcomes can make you focus too much on what can be assessed or described. This in turn makes the design of the teaching inputs very mechanistic and limits creativity and spontaneity. Even worse, outcomes-based teaching can remove an appreciation of the deeper values and meaning of the course, ignoring for example the affective domain described by Bloom (see Chapter 2).

There is truth in both these criticisms. However, our experience is that there are great benefits to be derived from this kind of planning, and if you put the needs of the learners at the heart of your work, the more profound issues are not ignored.

Writing aims, objectives and learning outcomes

How then should you approach writing aims, objectives and learning outcomes? The aim will often be easy to describe and may be one that has been set by someone else – for example if you have been asked to run a workshop by a teacher or colleague. Remember that the aim should explain the overall goal of the session in a clear and succinct way. It may be quite general in language and aspirational in purpose.

Objectives and outcomes should reinforce the aim and at the same time break it into specific, measurable elements. Try to make your objectives and learning outcomes both concrete and assessable. See the contrast in the lists of words in Table 5.1.

Table 5.1 Verbs you can use in writing aims, objectives and learning outcomes (expanded from D'Andrea, 1999, 51)

Aims	Objectives and learning outcomes
Know	Do
Understand	Analyse
Determine	Choose
Appreciate	Evaluate
Grasp	Use
Become familiar	Apply
	Practise

Table 5.2 shows an example of appropriate aims, objectives and learning outcomes for information skills.

Table 5.2 Aims, objectives and learning outcomes for legal information skills

Course

Legal information for first year law undergraduate students

Aim

To introduce students to the nature and structure of legal information and enable them to find cases, legislation and other legal material using print and electronic sources

Objectives
At the end of the session participants will:
• be able to find cases by name and subject using citators and Lexis
• be able to locate acts of parliament using *Halsbury's Statutes*
• be able to find legislation on a subject using *Halsbury's Statutes*
• be able to choose an appropriate source for each information requirement
• be able to use Lexis, Westlaw and Lawtel to find information
• use legal indexing tools to locate relevant and appropriate journal articles.

Remember that you can use external reference points when you set your aims, objectives and learning outcomes. Table 5.3 uses Bloom's taxonomy to organize the aims and objectives of a learning package.

Table 5.3 Bloom's taxonomy applied to an online induction package

Domain	Content area
Factual or knowledge-based	Orientation around library resources, linking to print and virtual within specific subject area(s) Access to passwords Information about borrower entitlements
Skills-based	Ability to search OPAC How to find relevant material in subject area Competence in using referencing conventions and techniques Experiment with different information search strategies and techniques
Affective	Develop self-reflection in information gathering Increase awareness of the need for the use of referencing conventions and standards Become aware of the range of choices in starting and information research project in terms of resources and techniques and apply them appropriately

Planning the inputs

The second stage in planning a learning and teaching experience is developing the content, planning the structure and producing learning materials. This will include:

* deciding on the content
* sequencing your topics
* preparing your teaching materials.

This stage combines pedagogical, professional and practical considerations. When drawing up your content you need to consider whether:

* it meets the needs of your learners
* it is current and professionally appropriate
* you have the resources to deliver it in the way that you wish and have planned.

There are several different approaches you can use in developing content.

Needs-based content

You might start from a purely needs-based assessment, talking to your learners about what they want to know and find out once you have established the aims and objectives. This can work well with adult learners, but the information universe can be so rich and complex that your students may not imagine what they might be able to discover unless you lead the way.

Assessment-led content

This is a much more directed approach of building a session around something required for an assessment or directly relevant to the workplace, derived from the knowledge you have acquired from auditing. A session on how to research a company for accountants, use legal information sources or look for recent articles on medical developments for health workers are examples. This is also the approach we use most often in our work in universities; after all, assessment defines the key elements of the curriculum.

Comparative content

Your third option is to think about the comparative needs of your group of learners. This is an approach used when organizing library induction sessions, basing planning on what we know new users need to know and looking at feedback from other groups we have already met. Remember that you should always audit your learners and be prepared to modify the content in response to feedback. For example ICT skills and experience can vary a great deal so do not assume what worked well with one group one year will work well a year later.

Information literacy and external definitions of content

Your last option is to plan the content around normative needs coming from external definitions. Your definitions may come from information literacy standards, the 'Big Six skills' (Eisenberg and Berkowitz, 1990), subject benchmarks (QAA, 2004), research methods modules, study skills, other curriculum requirements or the application of a specific methodology like critical appraisal (see Isabel's Case study 8 below).

Use of external standards must be explored when you are planning a longer programme or are integrating your input into a formal course, if only as a tool for critical review and reflection. Standards and guidelines will help you to define and develop specific objectives and learning outcomes and clarify your own planning.

Sequencing and structure

The standard way for structuring a learning and teaching event is through following what are known as the three Ps:

- Presentation the input from the tutor, usually in the form of a lecture or presentation
- *Practice* in a workshop, the hands-on element
- *Production* where the learner will be able to reproduce what has been learnt either within the session or outside.

This is used for all kinds of teaching and training activities and is a familiar and easy structure to follow. Remember though that you can adopt different approaches if you wish, perhaps reducing the amount of initial input or mixing presentation and practice, so there is talk, then a practical, then talk again, and so on.

The next stage is to decide upon how you will develop your presentation and learner discovery of the content. Ramsden (1992, 139) briefly mentions some of the main approaches, and we have illustrated this with some information skills examples:

- *Simple to complex* This is a tried and tested approach, for example if organizing training on how to search for information you begin with explaining how to conduct a basic search and finish with demonstrating advanced searching skills.
- *Particular to general* The best example here is to start by finding information on one subject and then demonstrating how this knowledge will transfer more widely.
- *Structure around enquiry* This is a problem-based or case study approach. You set the learners a problem and then use of resources is drawn into the more fundamental process of solving the problem.
- *Linear/chronological* You may use this approach when covering research sources, starting with how to find books and then moving on to other more current types of material.

Ramsden (1992) makes two very important points about the ordering of the content – that it should:

- be educationally justifiable
- make sense to a novice.

Sequencing and structuring needs to be thought of rather differently when you are preparing e-learning material. If you have produced something that learners can work through at their own pace and in their own time, you need to think about how the different elements work on their own and as a whole. As Laurillard (2002) suggests, different learners may find their own routes through the material. This means that they may not follow the logical structure that you had planned at the beginning.

Once you have decided upon the learning outcomes and the broad content you wish to include you then need to plan the learning activities necessary to meet your goals. On a practical level you should work out some timings and think about the materials you will need to achieve your learning outcomes. It is also a good idea to plot how you will assess whether each learning outcome has been achieved.

You may find it helpful to draw up a teaching or lesson plan such as the one shown in Table 5.4.

Table 5.4   Sample lesson plan

Learning outcome	Activity	Time	Material	Assessment
Choose a legal topic for information research and investigation	Lecture	10 minutes	Handout	Selection of keywords during practical
Use Lexis, Westlaw and Lawtel to find relevant legal information	IT practical	40 minutes	Worksheet; use of a computer	Completed worksheet

In the plan each learning outcome is linked to an activity; time is allocated; material requirements are specified and assessment is outlined.

Timing

Be flexible when you are planning your timings. Sessions will start later than you expect and activities always take longer than you have anticipated. It is a good idea to build some extra time into your teaching in case you overrun, either by adding in some specific 'overrun time' or making the session shorter than the total time allowed. Be generous in your timings for activities or put five minutes overrun time into your teaching plan. Equally, be careful not to rush the end of the session. Often information skills sessions are resource-centred. We are uncomfortable to spend time on anything other than demonstrating or using information resources. Yet, as we have argued throughout this book, beginnings and endings are important: tell the learners what they are going to know, let them learn it, and then tell them what they have learnt. This may be a paraphrase of a cliché, but it is still true. As we have stated before it can be helpful to divide your session into 15 or 20-minute blocks of time (Bligh, 1998).

Remember that the timings in your teaching plan are for your own use. If your learners have a session timetable, make their version less specific than your own detailed schedule.

Too much, too soon?

It is tempting to cram everything into your session, but try to resist this. Simplicity and clarity are all. Think about whether your learners need to know everything you are able to tell them, or whether you can identify what is sufficient for their needs. Try to think about making what you do say memorable, perhaps through sorting what you want to say into groups of three and building your teaching on three key points. Much of the time your information skills session will be a gateway into independent learning and research; your learners need starting points, not the last word.

Preparing teaching materials

You may have several options when it comes to preparing your teaching materials. Suitable resource materials may already be available, which you can use or adapt. These may be materials you have previously used that you can adapt or modify for different circumstances. If you do this, spend some time checking that the material is still current and appropriate for this group of learners. You could use materials prepared by colleagues, but remember the same considerations of checking for currency and relevance apply. A very efficient approach is to pool resources if you are doing a high volume of teaching, particularly if you are using a team for delivery. By developing and using shared materials you build a common pedagogical approach, reduce development costs and can involve everyone in the production process.

You could choose materials produced by a third party and available 'off-the-peg'. These may be commercially published guides or workbooks, materials from a database vendor or tutorials available on the web, like the Virtual Training Suite from the Resource Discovery Network (www.vts.rdn.ac.uk).

One of the drawbacks of this approach is whether these external materials meet the needs of your learners and are sufficiently motivating to your group of learners. 'Ready to use' materials are sometimes disappointingly generic and do not offer enough opportunities for local adaptation.

Remember that you can always adapt materials, perhaps using pre-existing materials as examples of good practice which you can modify for your own purposes. We consider this subject in more detail in Chapter 6.

Preparing for delivery

This is the third stage of planning. Squires (1994, 72) discusses the importance of the physical setting and how the space affects teaching by creating both opportunities and constraints. When you are planning your session think about how you would like to have the furniture arranged. These are some of the options:

- *Lecture style* Rows of chairs facing the front: best for formal presentations, demonstrations and whole-group teaching; we use this when we start and sometimes when we conclude a class.
- *Boardroom* Participants sit around a table: good for discussions, but less effective if you want to do a demonstration.
- *Workshop* Chairs arranged in a semicircle: good for collaborative work, and you can still separate yourself out as the workshop leader.
- *Group work* Chairs arranged around tables so that participants immediately start working in groups: can be problematic if you want to mix group work with whole-group teaching.

- *Laboratory* PCs arranged as a teaching space, either all facing the front or the side of the room: very good for hands-on IT but inflexible if you want to do anything else.

The layout and quality of the accommodation give clear messages about the nature of learning that will take place. In our experience the most flexible teaching room for classes is a flat space with network access, projection equipment and some computers. You have a variety of options for layout, formal and informal, and can integrate the use of computers in lecture or practical elements.

You also need to consider the kind of equipment you will use. As a minimum we think an overhead projector to show slides and a whiteboard or flipchart are essential. Remember that you can often reinforce what you are saying by writing down words or diagrams on the flipchart or whiteboard. Use of a data projector linked to the internet and PowerPoint is increasingly seen as standard but be careful that you do not let use of the technology overwhelm the message.

Although this may seem a minor point, make sure you have brought flipchart pens and whiteboard markers. These are often likely to disappear if left unattended in a teaching space.

E-learning

In our opinion there is no real distinction between preparing to teach in face-to-face and electronic environments, but there are notable theorists who would differ, particularly Salmon (2000) and Laurillard (2002).

Gilly Salmon (2000) defines a five-stage model of e-learning, which describes the stages that the learner goes through:

- access and motivation
- online socialization
- information exchange
- knowledge construction
- development.

This is a helpful description of a learner's experiences on an interactive e-learning programme, but we are not completely convinced by it as a new paradigm for learning. In Figure 5.2 we have tried to describe the e-learning environment.

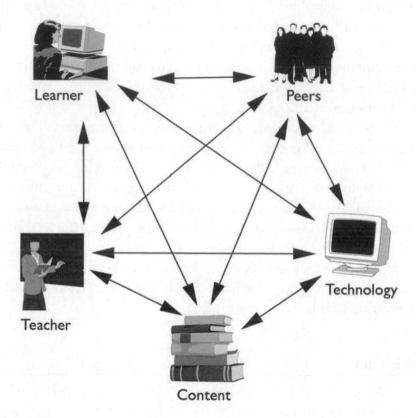

Figure 5.2 The e-learning environment

Apart from being technologically mediated how different is it from other learning opportunities? As a conventional teacher we might define our relationships in learning as shown in Figure 5.3.

Perhaps the difference is more to do with the level of control possessed by the tutor. In face-to-face learning environments, the tutor does not manage what happens during tea breaks, how learners use the library and so on. You may specify what the learners should do, and perhaps even make resources available to them, but you do not manage the whole of the learning universe.

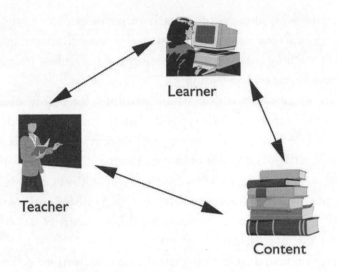

Figure 5.3 The traditional learning environment

Laurillard (2002) argues that although learning technologies are not individually capable of matching the effectiveness of the one-to-one teacher, together they can support the full range of students learning to acquire knowledge, for practice, discussion and discovery. She describes the iterative dialogue between learner and teacher, forming a conversational framework and how learning technology can sustain and extend that. Her *Rethinking University Teaching* is a widely influential text, but from our professional perspective, in common with many e-learning texts, it fails to recognize the role of independent study and research, so often mediated through the library. Nevertheless, it is essential reading should you wish to explore e-learning in more detail.

Finally, be aware that e-learning (or e-teaching) is not a single technologically mediated experience. Instead there are many different kinds of e-learning, ranging from a standalone interactive tutorial or e-mail-supported open learning to the much more immersive experience of an online conference. Salmon and Laurillard are both describing rich, interactive, assessment-bearing courses. We may not be involved in creating or delivering these kinds of programmes.

Your involvement in e-learning may be by getting involved in a purely online learning experience or as part of a blended course that mixes face-to-face with online learning. This may be based on campus or off-campus, linking groups who already know each other or people who have been strangers before. Your teaching role will also vary from publishing your face-to-face teaching material on a website, writing online learning activities to e-tutoring or e-moderating.

There are some differences between planning for online and planning for face-to-face teaching. We suggest this is because consideration of resources and technology becomes more integral in the planning and delivery rather than as a result of any qualitative difference in the nature of teaching and learning. It is likely that you will need to design your course inputs further in advance when teaching online, since you need to allow for time to write and test your material, particularly if you are going to carry out any assessment.

If you are interested in focusing on e-learning in more detail, we recommend that you look at *E-Learning and Teaching in Library and Information Services* by Barbara Allan (2002), which is an enthusiastic introduction to the subject with a wealth of practical examples.

Reflections and conclusion

Planning a teaching event can seem a contradictory process. As library and information professionals we want our learners to make the best use of libraries and information. We assume that as professionals we are also aware of the complex nature of their needs and wants, their skill levels and how psychological barriers to library and information use can be as formidable as physical or resource limitations. We must not let this knowledge make us lose focus in planning a learning and teaching experience. Paradoxically, perhaps, setting clear aims, objectives and learning outcomes will create a developmental structure from which our learners can construct their own understanding and knowledge.

There are many advantages of good planning. Both you and the learners know what is going to happen and what is expected; you have a good chance of having all the materials you need ready; and you can control your environment better or at least adapt to it if it is not ideal.

Bad planning can lead to you losing control of the learning and teaching experience. This may be through poor timing, so you finish frustratingly early or more commonly run out of time, missing out much of what you wished to cover. You are also at the mercy of the environment, and feel a victim when technology fails or the room is not set up correctly. You are also threatened by events – when things go wrong, or one of your learners is less co-operative than you expect. More seriously, bad planning can contribute to you having a set of learners who do not know or understand what you are trying to achieve, who feel confused and perhaps disenchanted.

We are not suggesting that every minute of a course or workshop should be planned in microscopic detail. You risk losing the spontaneity of some of the most enjoyable learning and teaching experiences and stifle the very independence you wish your learners to develop. Planning is a framework you can customize and personalize as you wish. Good planning, in Ramsden's words (1992, 141), is 'context-related, dynamic and experimental'. Without the structure from planning, learning and teaching will be shapeless, but you can determine the form yourself.

And make some time at the end of your event to reflect on what went right and what went wrong. The ability to reflect on action in order to engage in a process of continuous learning is another important skill for the effective teacher, which we discuss in Chapters 8 and 9.

Case study 7   Sorted for whizzy e-learning

Several years ago Stevie and some colleagues decided to create an interactive online tutorial on how to search the internet. Their decision to do this came less out of a learning and teaching mission than fear of being left behind because everyone else seemed to be creating this kind of resource.

It was generally felt that as well as the political benefit of catching up with external practice in the sector it would also be helpful to demonstrate internally the contribution that learning resources would play in online environments. Some of the people who taught information skills were also quite keen to have a tutorial that would cater for a wider range of learning styles and also help some self-directed study and practice in information retrieval.

The first meetings of the interested parties in the library were far from productive. It was difficult to reach any kind of shared agreement about how they should translate their current teaching materials and practice onto the web. The size of the group and the difference in opinions led to unfocused meetings and it was quite clear that a few people (not excluding Stevie) were getting a bit bored by the whole process.

Questions

1. What advice would you give to Stevie?
2. What might be suitable aims, objectives and learning outcomes for a tutorial on internet searching?

Discussion

The major problem that Stevie and his colleagues had encountered was that they were trying to translate what they already did, when they needed to start again. Stevie decided to establish a small project team, with just three people. The team members were Stevie himself, an IT person who was good at writing web pages and Clare, the graduate trainee. Clare was chosen because her colleagues thought that she would bring a fresh perspective: she hadn't spent so much time working in the library that she always thought like a librarian; she was still close to her inner student!

The project team had a first meeting and decided that they needed to go back to their learning outcomes and plan from there. The e-environment would mean they could take a fresh look at their learning outcomes and how they would deliver them. They would build the tutorial around three principles: it would be quick to do, interactive and relevant. They defined each aspect in more detail. It was agreed that the tutorial would take no more than 30 minutes to complete. Some parts would require the learner to type in text and search terms. Finally the learner must be allowed to follow through a search he or she wanted to do rather than be told exactly what to do at each stage. When Google became the search engine of choice there was another refinement: there would be no mention of Boolean searching because you didn't need to use it to get better results from Google.

The next stage was to think about how the team could contextualize the tutorial in specific subjects and they decided that they would build this element around essay questions. Learners would be asked to pick out the most important keywords and then search a live search engine using the words they had identified. The results would then be evaluated and a modified search attempted.

Clare had a lot of input at this stage, especially in helping to refine and clarify the language used. She ensured that the text was clear and simple and didn't rely too much on library jargon. She was also useful because although her searching was a bit more sophisticated than many new students at the time the project was developing, she was far from expert.

The tutorial was launched at the beginning of the academic year and was introduced to learners in information skills classes. Rather to Stevie's surprise it was heavily used within and outside the organization and computing students were required to complete it as one of their early coursework assignments.

Over the course of five years the tutorial was refined and modified. The biggest change was the switch from another search engine to Google but the principles remained unchanged. The fundamental objective was the development of effective searching skills, not how to use technology and, despite increasing familiarity with the internet, learners were not always better at finding the academic information they really needed. Finally, Stevie's department was seen as leading the way in e-learning – he even got asked to run workshops on e-tutoring for academic staff when he had never written a web page!

Case study 8   Information literacy through critical appraisal

Evidence-based medicine is becoming increasingly important within the National Health Service in the UK. It rests on the belief that medical practice can be improved by using and applying the results of health sciences research. As a result of this emphasis is increasingly placed on finding and applying research reported within the medical literature. This is context-specific advanced information literacy: finding, analysing and relating secondary data to real-life problems, combining understanding of the subject with a critical appreciation and application of the literature. In order to become effective practitioners of evidence-based medicine, health practitioners (especially doctors and nurses) must develop advanced skills in what is described as the critical appraisal – reading and reviewing mainly journal articles following a prescribed formula.

Isabel works as a medical librarian in a teaching hospital in the UK. In her previous post she was trained as a trainer in critical appraisal skills. She was rather dazzled when she went on her training course as she was the only information professional amongst lots of clinicians. She finished the course, but still felt a little cautious in applying all these new-found skills: would she be found out?

Questions

1. Do you think it is appropriate for library and information professionals to teach more fundamental information literacy skills like critical analysis and review? Provide a rationale for your answer.
2. Should Isabel carry on?

Discussion

Isabel worked alongside another information professional who had previously done the same course, and she realized that being an effective trainer in critical appraisal rested more on her skills as an effective facilitator and teacher than as a subject expert.

Critical appraisal courses rest on an established framework, which defines the main learning outcomes and methodology underpinning this approach. Isabel's role is therefore to ensure that these externally defined aims, objectives and learning outcomes are met. A validated checklist of question prompts (or 'review appraisal tool') is provided by the Critical Appraisal Skills Programme (CASP, 2004). The review appraisal tool is based around three fundamental questions:

- Is the study valid?
- What are the results?

• Will the results help locally?

The three fundamental issues are turned into ten question prompts (available from www.phru.nhs.uk/casp/reviews.pdf). Each prompt asks a straightforward question – 'Did the review ask a clearly focused question?' plus some additional prompts in this case identifying what exactly was meant by focused in terms of population, intervention or outcomes.

Thus the framework for the content is clearly defined. What Isabel must do is ensure that the learning and teaching event runs in such a way that participants can meet the learning outcomes. She achieves this through careful planning: choosing suitable articles, ensuring that the learners come from a single professional group (doctors and nurses might seek quite different evidence outcomes from an article on the treatment of palliative care, for example). Isabel also sends out learning materials in the form of selected journal articles to course participants before they attend the session. This in itself is quite different from the experiential approach usually adopted in information skills training courses.

Each of Isabel's workshops lasts for one and a half to two hours. In a typical session she might divide her class into several groups. Each group is asked to present a review of an article and to lead the comments and questioning on another group's presentation. The objectives have already been set in the critical appraisal methodology. The practical is the way in which the learning outcomes are met and are assessed within the session.

This is a very interesting approach. It extends the contribution of the information professional more deeply into what in a university we might define as the territory of the academic, that is reading and analysing content rather than finding it. However, the fundamental content is about the informational value of the material, and the questions prompt the critical evaluation skills that we aspire to achieve in the best of our own information skills teaching practice.

We must emphasize that this is a method that defines content and structure. As our case study has illustrated, questions of content are separate from the design of the delivery. Only when the two are combined appropriately with a suitable group of learners can the learning and teaching experience actually take place.

6 Delivery: tools, techniques and approaches

This chapter will discuss the actual delivery of your teaching. It will not, and cannot, provide you with a foolproof set of techniques and tricks for every occasion, but we hope to summarize some of the approaches you could adopt.

Each teaching situation is different: Geoffrey Squires' micro model of teaching and learning lists the key variables of rationale, content, process, level, participants, self and the physical, organizational and social setting and these make the difference between what works in one situation for one teacher and what fails for another (Squires, 1994). It is unlikely that we have complete control over all those variables. The room may be pre-booked for us, the groups too large or too small, the rationale for the teaching not fully explained and the content set.

However, there are key elements in delivering a successful teaching and learning experience that you should consider and apply whatever your context. Your teaching should encourage interaction between learner and teacher and between learners. It must be relevant and stimulate deep rather than surface learning. You should aim to control the learning environment, your performance and your tools but leave space for learners to challenge you and themselves. None of these things are easy, even for experienced teachers, but it is worth bearing in mind Ramsden's assertion that the content is the focus of the learning and the methods simply form the background (Ramsden, 1992). He maintains that there can never be a set of techniques that will ensure good teaching and learning but it is also true that bad teaching performance will override any amount of good planning, preparation and subject knowledge in the learners' mind. Simply think about your experiences of bad teachers to see the truth in this.

Although this chapter will concentrate on generic approaches to delivering a teaching and learning event it is perhaps worth looking at the range of options available to you. The flexibility you may have in delivery will often be predetermined by circumstances but there will often be some opportunity for you to choose between approaches. Wherever possible you should try to match delivery method to your learning outcomes. As we shall explore later in this chapter, some delivery methods are better at meeting particular types of learning outcomes than other ones.

This chapter must not be read in isolation, but studied in conjunction with Chapter 5 and Chapter 7. For effective teaching to take place you must start with the learning outcomes, then plan your assessment methods to test whether those learning outcomes have been achieved. Only then should you decide upon the delivery methods to aid the learner to succeed in the assessment and therefore achieve the learning outcome.

Teaching methods

Several teaching methods are described below but this is not a complete list of every option. There are excellent books by Gibbs and Habeshaw (1989) and Race (1999) to help you. However, these approaches are the most useful in our context.

Lectures

In British education to 'lecture' in any other context than education would have negative connotations (Light and Cox, 2001). To be expected to attend a lecture raises a level of expectation among your learners that this will be a passive experience for them, but there are still valid reasons why you might want to use at least some of your time in talking to the whole group. Lectures are a good way of coping with large numbers and a method of getting across background information or abstract concepts.

When delivering lectures remember to offer a change of some sort after 15 minutes or so. This could be moving from talk to demonstration, or asking the group to discuss something with their neighbours, brainstorming, showing a video or using a workbook. Your learners will probably be happy to coast through a lecture as it is a familiar and non-threatening experience for most of them. Try to challenge them and the format.

Seminars

A seminar is a form of small-to-medium-sized group teaching, built around discussion and the exchange of ideas. Seminars are generally more interactive than lectures but only really work well if the participants are able to make a contribution, usually by doing some advance preparation. Seminars are useful as part of a longer course but will rarely work as a single session, especially if you have had no contact with the participants before. They can be very valuable if you are looking at information skills as part of a wider information literacy course and want to explore the subject in more depth.

Workshops

Workshops are more active and participative than seminars and do not necessarily require preparation on the part of the participants. Workshops are the most commonly employed technique for teaching information skills since they allow learners to practise what they have learned within a supportive environment. They need careful planning as they require a hands-off approach for at least part of the time and this means setting tasks that are achievable by learners with a range of abilities. Within the workshop format remember that you have many options available in terms of structure and delivery: you can give your learners free choice in what they wish to do or plan a very clearly defined content.

Demonstrations

Demonstrations usually take place in conjunction with a lecture or workshop but they can make up a session on their own. Remember that they can be a passive experience for observers so try to find ways to include your learners in the demonstration in some way. If you are demonstrating a database let the learners set the agenda by asking them for topics to search rather than using a preprepared topic. Use one of the group to do the typing or keyboarding in order to engage the group's attention (and providing you the opportunity to break up that group sitting chatting at the back).

Tutorials

One-to-one or small group learning is often the most satisfying method of teaching as you can see more clearly when the learner grasps and applies what you say. The reference or enquiry desk is where we encounter this approach most often but many librarians will offer tutorial slots or have an open-door policy (under a variety of guises). You might also consider offering the one-to-one teaching after or alongside any formal group work to give learners the opportunity to clarify and reinforce the learning outside the more structured teaching environment.

Group work

Group work can be used outside the classroom or within a lecture, seminar or workshop. It is an excellent way to encourage peer learning, support and the development of social interaction, which can be important in motivating your learners. Effective group work does not come naturally to all, so ensure that you set aside some time for the group to form and regulate itself. You may need to establish some ground rules or principles for the group activity and as the tutor you need to decide what input you will provide yourself. If you are not sure about a larger group being able to break into workable sets then allocate the groups by numbering them or using 'red', 'amber' and 'green' to create three groups. During the group work be prepared to offer plenty of support to learners.

Questions will inevitably arise and frictions may develop. Be prepared for these, reiterate your objectives and be firm.

Peer learning

How often have you seen learners helping one another to use a database or find a piece of information? Encouraging this is an important element of teaching and you should try to include it in any plan. Inexperienced teachers will often see it as making them redundant but nurturing it, especially in a workshop, will produce excellent results and allow more experienced or advanced learners to stay focused. The best way to learn something is to teach it to others so it is beneficial to build peer learning in to your teaching strategy. Remember, also, that if you have met your learning outcomes your learners will be able to cascade their new-found knowledge and skills, so that a wider group than just the immediate attendees will benefit from your learning and teaching event.

E-learning

E-learning can have many different forms ranging from working through a computer-based learning package to live interaction in a chat room. Good e-learning puts the learner rather than the content at the centre of the learning experience. If well designed e-learning contains elements of lectures, seminars, workshops, tutorials, and group and peer learning. Your approach to e-learning should be no different from any other teaching method and certainly should not be defined by technology. Match the method to the learning outcomes and assessment but involve learners at every point; remember that they can walk away from the PC whenever they like.

Buzz groups

Buzz groups can be an effective way of breaking up a lecture, especially in a stepped or tiered room. Ask the learners to discuss something with the person sitting next to them, then with the pair sitting in front and so on.

Feedback on the main points of discussion can then be taken from a spokesperson of the larger group.

Poster tours

Posters can be particularly effective in a workshop when you have a small or medium-sized group. Write a series of questions or statements on separate sheets of flipchart paper and put them up around your room. Then break your learners into groups and move each group from poster to poster. Note their reactions and comments on the posters in order to build up a group-wide view. This is a simple and effective way of energizing a group, and an approach that will translate well into an online environment (although you would need to be more generous with your timings)! You might consider using a poster tour to get group input into constructing search strategies instead of demonstrating or brainstorming. You will need to decide on your level of interaction with the groups as they circulate, but some encouragement or stimulation of input may be needed if the group is unfamiliar with poster tours.

Games and simulations

Games could include role-play but this is not popular with most learners and should be used sparingly. Games can be useful in ice-breaking and could be used in information skills by creating a pub quiz atmosphere, with learners having to find information in teams. You should only use this sort of teaching method if you are well prepared and confident as it can descend into anarchy.

Brainstorming or free discussion

Brainstorming is useful in energizing a group but have some options ready yourself to stimulate ideas. Be careful to use the ideas or keywords that you garner from the group. Learners will be more prepared to take part in any exercise if they can see an immediate value in it.

How to underpin good teaching

Although the methods used in teaching are obviously important it is per-haps more useful to concentrate on the issues that should underpin the selection and delivery of those methods and it is these that we will now consider.

Make your teaching a conversation

Ramsden's (1992) assertion that good teaching should be a conversation between learner and teacher encapsulates much of our philosophy of teaching, but this is not easy to achieve in practice. We often think that we have a mass of information to impart to our learners, all of which seems vital to their understanding of the subject, and only an hour in which to do so. Providing this mass of knowledge through a lecture or structured task seems to be the safest, most complete method of delivery. We could include a demonstration but really there is insufficient time to allow much more than a few questions at the end of the session.

This methodology is attractive, especially to new and inexperienced teachers, because it gives you complete control over the material. There is a pleasing sense of power through being in control of your subject and it is true that the lecture offers an effective way of covering large amounts of material. However, as Bligh (1998) notes, the lecture is not effective at promoting thought and changing attitudes and it is these elements that lie at the heart of learning.

For your teaching to be a conversation you will need to listen, and respond, to the learners. This calls for sympathy on your part towards individual and group dynamics. As with any conversation you should avoid sarcasm and irony (used appropriately and with caution) until both sides understand and feel comfortable with each other. The information you impart should be organized and coherent to allow the learners to respond in a similar fashion. Look again at the material you want to cover and trim it to its core elements to allow time and space for your teaching to be challenged and be ready to answer questions like 'Why?' and 'So what?' (Race, 1999). There is little use in covering a mass of material if your learners have not listened or understood any of it so allow them to question you either throughout the learning experience (especially when working with individuals or small groups) or during set slots (perhaps better with large groups). In the latter use buzz groups to come up with questions, especially if the group is very large or you fear that peer pressure will result in silence.

In making your teaching a conversation you should be prepared to respond to the needs of the group and amend your plan for the session accordingly. This can make the session a satisfying two-way learning experience. You can explore how information skills are perceived and used in context during the conversation and match delivery to expectation and need. However, your teaching may stray into areas that were not included as part of your original plan. As long as you recognize the risks of being sidetracked this is no bad thing. A conversation follows a mutually understood and agreed agenda and your teaching should allow the learners to interject their concerns and ideas. Allowing them the space to do so and encouraging them when they do will enrich the teaching for them and for you.

Be conscious of the language you are using. Try to produce simple, clear and unambiguous instructions, and illustrate, spell out and write down any complicated terms. Remember that terms like OPAC may mean something to you, but are meaningless to most learners. Some people will ask for clarification if they do not understand something; more people will not ask for fear of being made to appear foolish. This is even more important if you are working with people whose first language is not English. Try to use shorter and clear sentences and avoid too many metaphors: they do not always translate! Be conscious of intercultural dimensions when developing your conversation. If your learners do not have the same understanding of the rules of discourse as you do you might end up in a slightly different place from where you had planned!

Encourage deep not surface learning

We have mentioned deep and surface learning in Chapter 2. Your teaching methods should aim to get beyond surface learning and encourage a deeper understanding.

Many learners will come to information skills sessions thinking that they are already perfectly competent at finding and using information. Others will come wishing simply to know how to use a particular database or get a specific piece of information and think they don't need to know more. Your teaching should challenge these ideas and allow the learner to get beyond the surface to understand the underlying principles of information creation, organization and delivery. There is often a concentration in information skills sessions on the practical issues: the issuing of passwords, the correct keys to use or which database to use in which context. These are important but can usually be achieved through a handout, website or exercise. Try to challenge your learners at the start of the session. Show, in a sympathetic way, how much they don't actually know in a real situation or case study. This doesn't mean that you should try to humiliate them but rather talk them through a real example, comparing how they would tackle it with how you would. Use poster tours or group work to come up with innovative strategies for dealing with a problem. If learners have strategies that work then make sure that they know why they work and use this to explore other situations that they could encounter. This approach is most effective in a workshop but can also be used in very small or very large groups.

Make your learning active

Active learning should mean more than simply inserting an activity into your teaching. Most authorities agree that after 15 or 20 minutes a new stimulus is required by learners if they are to maintain concentration. This could be in the form of a database demonstration or a quick brainstorm of keywords before settling back into your talk. These are useful but they are not active learning for this requires that the learners think about their learning in context.

In many educational systems there is cultural resistance to active learning. Students expect to be told the answers and may resist when asked to participate in their own learning. Overcoming this cultural barrier can be difficult but clear explanations of the learning outcomes and expectations do much to lessen resistance.

A popular and effective way of introducing an active element into your teaching is through group work. Vygotsky (1978) argued that learning is highly dependent on social interaction and encouraging your learners to work with others to solve problems will minimize passive acceptance of the teacher–learner relationship. Group work is influenced by many factors: the previous experiences of group work by the learners, the cultural context, the pre-existing relationship, if any, of learners with their colleagues and the design of the exercise that you are asking of them.

In most information skills teaching the group is liable to form and interact only within the confines of the session. Try to break the existing pattern of relationships by organizing the groups yourself. A good way of doing this is by counting the learners into numbered groups, so that people are mixed together more. If possible involve some form of physical movement to energize the groups, which is a potentially lengthy operation in large or stepped rooms, so build in time. Groups of four are probably best as they are small enough to prevent anyone being able to hide and yet allow differences of opinion and debate to surface.

As with all learning make the activity relevant and stimulating. You might want to create a jigsaw classroom where groups are given different elements of a problem to solve before coming together to complete the solution. This involves each group finding information from different sources to complete an assignment and then commenting on the search techniques and sources they have used.

Your role in the process should not be completely passive. The task should be explained clearly and monitored as the groups work. You may need to keep discussions on track or stimulate groups to begin work; there is often an awkward moment at the start when no one wishes to start the activity. Move around and between the groups and take the psychological temperature of the session. You may need to stand back or release tension, elicit opinion or add an example to the discussion but you should take an active interest in the activity. Try to set ground rules in the group brief and then stick to them, in particular timings for tasks. Give clear announcements about how long the groups have left to complete their activities and stop on time.

Try to allow rewards for individuals and groups especially if formal assessment is involved. However, even if not assessed then praise groups and recognize individual input equally. The most common cause of discontent with group work is the feeling that it is not fair and you should be aware that some individuals will make a more substantial contribution than others.

Make the learning relevant

Ramsden (1992) makes the very important point that 'sound teaching strategies encourage students to relate to the subject matter they are studying in a purposeful way'. To many learners their interaction with the library is an extra burden, something to be endured as a distraction from their real studies or interests. You will need to combat this belief by constantly and explicitly linking your teaching with the internal learning outcomes of the session and the learner's wider context. Relate your teaching to real and meaningful examples and try to match the culture of the learners. This means not just using appropriate examples, but also consider your use of language and the level of formality with which you address people.

Be aware of the dangers of trying to be something that you are not. Cultural reference points are constantly shifting and references to music or popular culture can misfire if you are not completely sure of your ground. Try to understand the pedagogy of the wider subject and to work with it. This could mean that you use a case study approach with law or business students, evidence-based learning with nurses or problem solving with scientists. There are cultural and disciplinary conventions: in our own teaching we use quite different reference points when we work with international and UK students or people from different subject areas. Whatever your approach learners will respond to familiar methodologies and be more receptive to your particular message.

Make your teaching a performance

Although this book never intended to include presentation skills it is important to recognize what Milne and Noone (1996) call the micro-skills of teaching. Without the ability to engage your learners, to make yourself heard and understood, to interact positively with the environment and learning materials and to keep learners' attention and interest until the end of the session you will struggle to achieve your desired outcome. It is also important to recognize that although you may have already delivered the same session many times before, perhaps even several times that day, or that you may be feeling tired or run down, it will be a unique experience for the learners. Respect your learners and make each session a performance of which you are proud.

This does not mean that you need to be a consummate actor to be a good teacher. You will achieve much through good preparation and planning allied to the ability to think clearly and react to circumstances as they occur. However, there are 'tricks' that can help make the learning more effective:

- Try to start well. Engage attention by a shout, bang the door and so on and then make sure that your first sentence is clear, welcoming and warm.
- Don't tell jokes unless you are a comedian.
- Speak clearly. Test your clarity by video or asking a colleague to observe you.
- Speak in sentences and speak precisely. Do your best not to let your sentences fade away. It is hard for anyone to understand half-sentences and vague phrases – and even worse for people whose first language is not English.
- Signpost your way through the session. When you are moving onto a different topic, make this clear to the learners. The clearer you make the structure of the session, the clearer it will be for learners to understand.
- Watch your speed. Most of us speed up at the start and end of a session. Be aware of this and listen to yourself.
- Be comfortable. Wear appropriate clothes but make sure they fit you well.
- Don't be afraid to make mistakes. You can think about avoiding them later but try not to worry about them at the time of the session.

- Start with relatively simple ideas and build up to the difficult, more complex issues.
- Try to end the session on time or even early (as long as you have covered the material no one will complain about an early finish).
- End the session by telling learners where they can find help.

Practice improves performance, as does reflection on feedback (see Chapter 8) but each time you interact with learners remember that what you say should be fresh and interesting for them. Peterson (1992) has some helpful advice on this topic.

Give learners something to take away

Race and Brown note that deep learning rarely happens in the formal learning session so you should always endeavour to give learners something to take away from your learning and teaching event. This can include a handout but could be a chance to apply their new skills or knowledge practically, a desire to find out more or a changed attitude to the subject (Race and Brown, 1998). Learning is consolidated if used soon after exposure and this means that timing of the session is an important element in learning and the reason why the familiar UK higher education model of teaching information skills during the first week of student life usually fails.

It is usual for teachers to provide handouts, sometimes as documents given out in the session but increasingly in electronic formats (web or CD). Well-structured handouts that reinforce learning can be helpful but often they are no more than a copy of the slides used in the session. These may offer little without the attendant commentary, although video or web-based software can allow this to be included. If you distribute handouts try to make them interactive in some way. Include space for notes, miss elements out to encourage learners to add material in their own words and try to vary presentations to account for more visual learners. Diagrams, pictures or video can help with this.

Be prepared to provide material in different formats for those learners who could not otherwise access it in print. Consider audio handouts and if you use print follow available guidelines on font, text size and layout to help those with dyslexia or a visual impairment. When using web-based or other electronic media make sure that it satisfies or exceeds the requirements of relevant standards, for example Bobby (n.d.) and Betsie (BBC Education, n.d.).

Think as well about when you will distribute your handouts – at the beginning or end of a session or at specific intervals? If you are providing several handouts, it can sometimes be helpful to create information packs, but you may need to decide which approach will best reinforce your teaching. Do not just leave these decisions to chance.

Make the environment work for you

The learning environment is often the one element we cannot influence as we are timetabled or limited by the availability of rooms. However, this environment can have a major effect on the quality of the learning experience – remember Herzberg from Chapter 3! Few can work effectively in overheated or cold rooms, or if they are crowded. The best planned practical workshops can fail if the computers are not available or will not run the relevant software. The layout of the room will play a key role in the interaction between teacher and learners and between learners. For example, a simple thing like fixed chairs can make group work difficult to organize.

You should try and influence the environment wherever possible. Librarians are often not good at being assertive but if for example you need computers to make the session work then you should try to get a room that offers them. Take a professional approach to your teaching and don't accept the commission for a session if you cannot deliver it properly. Try to see the room you will use before the session and decide what seating arrangement you want in advance. Most people will try to sit in the middle or at the back of a set of seats and with small group sizes this can mean that your audience is sitting a long way away from you. In this case try to arrange the front seats in a horseshoe and ask the students to sit there. No one will be sitting 'at the front' any more than anyone else. If this is impossible try to include some activity that means the students are moved around and encourage groups to work in areas that bring them closer to you or move to them.

Always have reserve strategies and tools to cope with environmental problems. This could include having slides as well as a computer-based presentation or having an activity in hand that doesn't require mass movement.

Although most teachers will be prepared to work within the constraints of their environment also be ready to abort the teaching if it is clearly impossible to deliver it successfully. One of your authors was once faced with over 50 students in a room holding 20 and with youthful optimism attempted to continue. It was not a success.

Control the situation

Control of learners is as important as control over the environment. This does not mean that you should try to rule your learners through fear but is recognition that learning cannot take place in chaos. You should be prepared to make difficult decisions as you teach in order to maintain order and encourage learning.

You should not be prepared to tolerate disruptive behaviour. Make this clear early on and act immediately on those, thankfully rare, occasions when it occurs. Be firm with learners who have agendas other than your intended outcomes and try to keep potentially disruptive negotiations with them outside the session.

Control is also about being prepared to let go of the learners within your framework. For inexperienced teachers this can be frightening and the reason that they will often fall back on the lecture format. As long as you have clearly explained what is required and set explicit ground rules then there should be no problem. Move around and intervene where necessary, but being able to let go of the formal teaching position at the front of the class can be a liberating experience for teacher and learner.

Use teaching aids

Few people can hold the attention of learners without some form of visual aid. Listening to one voice without another form of stimulus will almost certainly induce boredom in your audience for all but the most charismatic speaker. Most of us use a variety of teaching aids including PowerPoint or overhead slides, video, workbooks, large screen demonstrations or web-based tutorials (supervised or outside the classroom). All of these have their place in teaching and can, if used well, enhance the learning experience.

Some words of caution are appropriate though. Teaching aids can be used as an obvious prop rather than as a support tool. They must play an integral role in learning or they will be rejected by your learners. This is often true of PowerPoint or OHP slides, which can just be text-heavy reiterations without any true purpose or value. Try to keep your slides to a minimum with no more than eight lines and between ten and 20 words maximum. Make them clear and consistent, use primary colours and show them to illustrate your points. We tend to keep distractions like cartoons, animations and reveal features to a minimum. They usually add little and serve only to distract and irritate, but those of you more comfortable with visual learning and teaching may wish to use them.

Technology should never lead or define the content. When using visual aids remember to refer to them but continue to talk to your audience rather than at the screen (this is a common and very irritating habit). Involve learners in the presentation by asking them to fill in blanks or add to slides.

Expect any technology to fail (wherever you work) and have alternatives ready. These can be printouts, alternative activities or OHPs instead of PowerPoint presentations. Set aside some time ahead of the beginning of your class and load any presentation on to the computer in advance or have it attached to an e-mail that you can access via the web rather than trust to an easily corruptible disc drive. It can also be a good idea to check any web pages you are planning to use, just to ensure that they will display on a different computer, and have not been blocked by an institutional firewall or require software that is not supported on that computer.

Finally, remember to bring along any materials you might need, including flipchart markers, sheets of paper and pens.

Is e-learning different?

We have not differentiated face-to-face teaching and learning events from e-learning in this book as we feel that the basic principles of good teaching apply as much in the virtual arena as they do in the physical classroom. Neglect of these principles and the seductive powers of technology mean that much of what is called e-learning is simply poorly transferred material from a face-to-face session and this rarely works in practice.

As Race and Brown (1998) point out, good e-learning is learning not content driven, student centred not system driven. Sadly this is often not the case in practice. Institutional, government and market forces have led to the rush to transfer learning opportunities online without also allowing for the development time needed to create effective e-learning environments. Race (1999) estimates that it takes some 100 hours of development time to produce one hour of e-learning but this time is rarely made available.

All of the issues covered in this chapter are as appropriate to e-learning as they are to face-to-face teaching. The learning should be relevant, active and allow interaction between learners and between teacher and learners. Environmental issues should be considered, for instance whether the activity created on one system will work on another, or if the load time will be acceptable on a home computer on a telephone compared with a networked machine in your workplace. Facilitating discussions is as demanding as controlling a classroom and teaching aids need to be carefully considered and planned. Using web-based learning can be stimulating and exciting but only if sound pedagogical practice is applied. E-learning is a different delivery method but the same principles of good teaching apply.

Conclusion

There is no magic formula that allows you to match the perfect delivery method to particular circumstances. There are far too many variables for that ever to be the case and most of us make compromises every time we teach. However, the guiding principle should always be to choose the most appropriate delivery method available to achieve the desired learning outcome. In deciding on your methods be aware of your environment, the learners and your own strengths and weaknesses but don't compromise on this fundamental issue.

Case study 9 Technophobes versus computers: an alternative approach

Pauline Cook is the academic librarian responsible for health and community studies at a medium-sized university. She enjoys working with her diverse learner community. Students range from school leavers to many mature entrants coming from very different backgrounds. The variety is not just in age or ethnic group but also in the kinds of courses students are studying, covering everything from full-time undergraduate and postgraduate courses to part-time programmes of all kinds of length and level.

There is one thing that many of the students have in common: a rather unexpected reluctance to use computers. Pauline had a couple of near-disastrous workshops with social workers in which everyone seemed to go away unhappy.

It had all started so well. Pauline had negotiated with the course leader, Dave Wagstaff, to have three one-hour timetabled sessions over three weeks with a group of about 16 learners. She planned the weeks following a tried and tested format. In week one they would look at how to find books, moving on to using bibliographic databases in week two and finishing with internet searching in the last week. Each session would follow the same kind of tripartite structure of presentation, practice and production. Pauline would introduce the aims, objectives and learning outcomes for the session and review the key resources or approaches. The learners were then given a worksheet and a task to complete. Each week was designed to build on from the previous one, and the tasks increased in complexity and the amount of autonomous learning that needed to take place. Pauline was quite pleased with this plan, which was clearly relevant to the needs of her learners.

When the time came, the sessions started to unravel. Some of the students were very reluctant to use the computers and asked such basic questions that Pauline wasn't able to cover all the ground she had planned in either the first or second week. The amount of remedial help she was giving interfered with her intended learning outcomes and by the end of the third week most of the students didn't appear to be any more knowledgeable about or comfortable in using the electronic information resources that were relevant to their studies. Pauline had been careful in her auditing and had included activities in the first two weeks that required plenty of peer interaction and support, so she was very disappointed.

Questions

1. What was the underlying reason for Pauline's difficulties?
2. How can Pauline change her delivery?

Discussion

Pauline made a simple but fundamental mistake in underestimating the level of technophobia among her learners. By building each session around the use of computers she failed to meet her intended learning outcomes, which were less about using technology than the ability to find information effectively.

The next time she was asked to run the same sessions (apparently she had been more critical of their success than Dave Wagstaff or most of the students) she revised her lesson plans completely. She realized that she needed to shift from a resource-centric approach to modelling through her learners' information needs and their information-seeking behaviour.

In the first session Pauline decided that she would focus on analysing topics so participants would have thought through problems and the kinds of information they needed before going to use the computers. She devised a poster tour, with four different problems written up on flipcharts. One was about adoption and fostering, the second child protection, the third mental health and the final one anti-social behaviour orders. These were all topical issues relevant to participants' work and each would require learners to use a range of different information sources ranging from the library catalogue to journals and official publications.

During the first session the students, in groups of four, toured around the posters, adding keywords and additional questions to clarify or focus the topic further. There was plenty of active learning in evidence and a lot of interaction between the groups.

The next week Pauline brought along the notes from the poster tour and set the learners off to explore what they could find on the different topics. They still worked in groups although they were quite unstructured. Individuals or pairs might go and use the computers, and there was certainly a lot of peer tutoring. Because everyone had a set of keywords and questions they didn't flounder in the same way as they had before, even though Pauline still spent plenty of time showing them how to log on to the relevant databases.

The third week was built around evaluating the material found on the basis of its currency, accuracy and relevance, plus some tips for referencing and citation.

At the end of the course, Pauline was much more confident that the learning outcomes had been met. By concentrating less on technology and the names of specific resources, the learners had actually been able to find and use information much more analytically.

[Note: this discussion is based on the approach adopted by Heather McBryde-Wilding at University College Northampton; the description of the problems encountered is our own.]

Case study 10   Online delivery of information

Intranet delivery of everything was very much the flavour of the month in the government library where John worked as an information librarian. The library manager was keen to develop his section's presence on the web pages, not just by developing virtual enquiry and support services but by encouraging increased end-user access to resources. As their section was closely involved in most of the knowledge and information management initiatives this was not particularly difficult to achieve.

In addition to desktop delivery of resources and some innovative approaches to enquiry handling the information team was keen to use the intranet for open-access learning and staff development. As a first stage, training guides from database suppliers were mounted on the intranet pages, with some instructions on how to access and use named resources.

Questions

1. Do you think this is an appropriate approach?
2. What could John do instead?

Discussion

The problem here is that an information resource has been created rather than a learning resource. Little thought has been given to the learning outcomes for anyone using these guides and there is no assessment, tutor mediation or opportunity for group learning.

When there is limited time to develop learning resources it can be very easy just to dump material onto an online learning environment and assume that because it can be accessed from a computer you have created an e-learning resource. At the same time, it is important to be aware that very few people would complete tutorials on using a particular resource without some kind of real and expressed need. John and his colleagues need to think about how they can encourage people to use their online training resources. They have several options.

In the first instance they perhaps need to think about revising the way they are presenting and promoting the materials. First they should consider whether the tone, style and presentation are right. Perhaps the materials could be revised to reflect frequently asked questions rather than 'A quick tour around Database X'. Alternatively, perhaps the materials need to be made more interactive, with quizzes and assessment activities.

Secondly, the team might reflect on how their online training relates to the section's objectives. John and his colleagues could think about marketing the materials, perhaps linking availability of these materials to other promotions or supplier presentations, for instance 'Spotlight on Y' with presentations (and even free gifts) from Database Y's suppliers.

Thirdly, the team could explore the possibility of strategic integration with human resources and the general departmental staff training programme. This has much potential, both as a way of shifting the focus of training from being library-based to a corporate activity, and even in the possibility of linking completion of materials with some form of CPD credit. In this way, instead of being used as a resource designed for individuals to work through in isolation, materials could be used to create a more interactive online course that also includes opportunities for social interaction and group learning.

Case study 11   Lecture or show: an innovative approach to working with a large group

How can we make library induction interesting for students? Nearly every academic librarian wonders whether they could be doing something more innovative when faced by a sea of blank faces at the beginning of the academic year. Our difficulty is caused by lack of time and resources: often too many new students and insufficient time and space to do more than give a large-group lecture. We all have horror stories. The student who spent an hour staring at the floor or the ceiling, another one who fell asleep, or the early morning session the day after the freshers' disco when those who managed to turn up kept running out to be sick.

Even worse is the dreary repetition of rules and regulations. You know your students need to take in the information, and that they are more likely to remember it if they are told and shown rather than just being given a handout. At the same time you empathize with their boredom: why at the very beginning of a new stage in their life do they have to sit and be so passive, listening to speaker after speaker covering procedures and describing services when there is so much out there to experience? Yet in order to understand university life the learners need to know about the rules, expectations and how things happen.

In many universities at least some library inductions are based entirely in a classroom or lecture theatre. They are usually built around a presentation about the role of library and information services in the student experience. There might be demonstrations of the online catalogue, databases or an induction video. Sometimes tours are offered, although they are not always logistically possible: tours for 300 students are not very easy to organize in an afternoon!

Now we are aware that there is a lot of good practice particularly when you are working with smaller groups, but this mass approach is still very common.

Question

1. What suggestions do you have for making library induction a more engaging and interactive experience?

Discussion

A lot of texts on how to teach in higher education address the topic of making large-group teaching more effective. The most common suggestions are:

*   to design an effective structure with pace and variety
*   to introduce interactivity through using questioning, making a student a guinea pig at the keyboard or group work
*   to add a practical element
*   to teach in a team so the learners hear a variety of voices and approaches.

Nigel and his colleagues used a number of these approaches to develop what is a genuinely innovative treatment of library induction for groups ranging in size from 30 to 300 new students. Their approach, which they dubbed the Cephalonian method, combined a number of approaches:

*   audience participation
*   appeal to more senses through using music and colour
*   humour
*   risk and variety for those involved in delivery.

Audience participation was achieved by handing out question prompt cards to students at the beginning of the session. Each card had a question like 'How do I find the books on my reading list?', covering all the main points that new students would need to know, ranging from opening hours, photocopying and printing, library rules and regulations to the names and contact information for the subject librarians.

The prompt cards were in different colours. Blue cards had basic introductory information, yellow had contact information, red cards had information on services and green cards had miscellaneous information. The session was structured so that blue, then yellow, red and finally green card questions were asked. (And in case anyone was colour-blind the colour of the card was printed near the question as well.)

The session leader would ask for a 'blue card' and so on but would have no control over the order in which each question was asked. This added an element of unpredictability and variety for those involved in delivery. Each question had a matching (coloured) slide with the answer to the questions.

There were two other elements to the approach. One was that the questions were sometimes a little unusual, for example, 'My Mum's e-mailed me a photo of Miguel, my pet iguana. Where can I print him out?' The second was that music was played at the beginning, end and when students were asked to fill out worksheets.

Library staff and students seemed to enjoy the induction. Learner feedback was very positive, with 97% of respondents saying it was an effective introduction to the library.

This is a theatrical and creative approach and worked very well because of good preparation and the enthusiasm of the library staff delivering it. There are several possible modifications: using the question and answer prompts when running a library tour, converting the whole process into an online exercise, and so on, but fundamentally we have a fresh way of making lectures interesting and informative.

[*Note: the inspiration behind the second real-life case study in this chapter is the work of Nigel Morgan and Linda Davies at Cardiff University. Our thanks to them for letting us describe what they do as an example of what we think is best practice and innovative delivery.*]

Case study 12   Information skills and outreach

As well as running information skills programmes within the setting of a hospital or medical education, a number of library and information professionals are also involved in outreach training and development activities to community health workers. This is Flora's current occupation. As an outreach librarian she is responsible for document supply, literature searching and workplace training for mental health workers, general practitioners and other health service staff.

Questions

1. What kinds of problems might Flora encounter?
2. What would you suggest she might do?

Discussion

Flora has little control over the kind of teaching environment she will be using, and has found that this can vary from a seminar room filled with 25 people and a data projector to an informal training session in a corner of a doctor's surgery or someone's office. In fact she usually prefers the smaller group work because she can build her session more directly around learners' needs. Nevertheless, the unpredictability of her environment means that Flora needs to be flexible and adaptive in the approaches she takes to delivery.

At the moment the most common pattern is that someone will contact Flora to arrange a training session. She does a fair bit of marketing to promote her outreach and training work and is in the happy position of arranging her sessions in response to definite approaches from interested groups. Before she goes out to give a session, Flora likes to find out a little bit about the place and the people she will be visiting.

She has found for instance that it can be easier to run sessions for single professional groups: all doctors or all nurses, for example. In part this is because she can emphasize slightly different sources like Medline as opposed to Cinahl, but also the two professional groups behave in slightly different ways. The doctors are often very specific; they like to know how to find an answer, and they might do some window shopping to see what different databases have to offer on a very specific topic. Nurses on the other hand like to discuss and chat about what they are doing; social learning is important to them. They will often have a research question as well, sometimes linked to some of the compulsory CPD they are undertaking at any given time, but their focus is often more social scientific than the doctors' medico-scientific perspective.

Although the tone and culture of the workshop might be different, Flora aims to cover the same underlying principles in every session. Each time she will start by using a question or topic that participants have themselves identified, and then work through the principles of effective database searching, ranging from keywords, use of controlled vocabulary, combining terms, downloading, accessing the full-text and so on. Flora is always prepared to modify her content either to meet the needs of her learners, perhaps covering more basic IT principles like introductory e-mail, and reducing the scope of the session to ensure that the fundamental learning outcomes are met. In general she finds that she can be more flexible when working with smaller groups. With her bigger classes she usually has a more rigid structure, even though there is always scope for individual enquiries and support.

As well as being flexible in planning her learning and teaching events, Flora also makes sure that handouts are provided. She knows that some people will go away and work through the materials, and that just providing something on paper will reinforce the learning outcomes from the session. Assessment in these sessions is usually informal: learning is tested by doing, and of course follow-up training and support are always available.

This case study exemplifies that delivery does not just take place inside a classroom, but how someone with well-developed skills as a teacher and learning facilitator can go out and help learning to happen anywhere. This is not an entirely casual process. Flora is a confident trainer, and has a lot of understanding of and sympathy with her learner community. She is able to merge her training skills with her expertise as a health information professional to support effective, contextualized learning events for people who would otherwise find it difficult to attend courses run on-site.

7 Assessment

We will now turn to the question of assessment. First of all we will review what we understand by assessment and how it fits into the learning and teaching process. We will then discuss some assessment principles before turning to how we can use different assessment methods in teaching and supporting information skills development.

As in many other parts of this text we need to be conscious of our own cultural and intellectual assumptions. We are presenting to you perspectives on assessment that are orthodoxy in British and other English-speaking universities. We believe the same points apply to most of our teaching and learning support work in all contexts, but nevertheless some of you reading this text may disagree; we welcome your views!

Understanding assessment

For many of us assessment is viewed at a distance from the teaching experience. We sometimes can recall having taken tests and exams some time after we learnt the original content, often in a different physical location with the process administered and assessed by strangers. The process of assessment has been separated from the learning experience and so we tend to view them as discrete activities.

Yet assessment should be seen as an intrinsic part of the learning and teaching continuum. Assessment is the way that you can test whether your learning outcomes have been achieved. You have choices in the nature of assessment you use – and we will explore them in detail later in this chapter – but to be relevant and meaningful to the teacher and to the learners assessment needs to link to your aims, objectives and learning outcomes.

When you are teaching information skills you will often find that your best ways of assessing learners will be within the learning and teaching experience. Assessment takes place through your learners doing practical work and you giving feedback to them on their performance. You may not be allocating marks or grades, but it is still assessment.

In fact, we believe that assessed work is important for your learners. There is much discussion about whether learners will only do work which is assessed (see Chapter 3) but, more fundamentally, assessment provides a chance for the learners to engage directly with the learning opportunity by turning the information they have been given from your teaching into an embedded personal knowledge and practice.

Defining assessment

Before we go any further it will be helpful to discuss some definitions of assessment and key issues related to it.

Most teaching and learning texts will tell you that there are two fundamental types of assessment. The first is called summative assessment, which you can characterize as the assessment that decides whether you pass or fail and what mark you receive. Summative assessment usually takes place at the conclusion of your learning experience, most frequently in the form of a final exam or some other test. The second type is called formative assessment, which gives you feedback and helps you to develop and improve your work. Formative assessment always takes place while you are doing your course. Many teaching programmes combine formative and summative assessment within a course or curriculum. Formative and summative are very useful definitions, but there are some other ideas we need to explore.

Traditionally, in most schools and universities assessment is used as a tool to separate out and distinguish between individual learners. It is expected that not everyone will get the highest marks, and in fact there will be a normal distribution of marks along a bell curve, so that a few people get very high or very low marks and the rest are distributed in the middle. Grades might be 'norm referenced' so that assessment decisions are made only in comparison against the whole range. In the UK this is often used in public examinations when it is decided that x% will get the highest grade, and the mark threshold for that grade is decided when all the results have been analysed. Biggs (2003) describes this as a 'measurement model of assessment'.

There is an alternative assessment model. In criterion-referenced assessment, performance is checked against the learning outcomes. The assessment decision is based on the extent to which those learning outcomes have been met, and graded accordingly. Biggs (2003) calls this a 'standards model of assessment'. Standards (or what we have called objectives in Chapter 4) are turned into learning outcomes and become the benchmark for assessment.

There is still great variation in practice even using this model. Some teachers apply this in a way that means most students will be able to meet the standards. Marks or grades may be abandoned in favour of simple pass/fail decisions. Assessment is used to encourage learners to reach the levels of competence. Alternatively this same criterion-referenced approach can be used in grading, when you make assessment judgements based on the level or extent to which the learning outcomes have been met. And in any case, in our experience, even in this approach your marks will still probably be scattered across the bell curve because of the differences between your learners.

Biggs also discusses what he terms authentic or performance assessment. By this he means opportunities for learners to demonstrate actively what they know rather than a passive retelling of the facts they have been told. This is an important definition for assessment for teaching information skills. What you should seek to do is provide opportunities for your learners to learn and do rather than demonstrate recall. For example, even in something like a library induction we suggest it is more useful for your learners to know how to find our how many books they can borrow than to be able to parrot the loan entitlements back to you.

There are two other assessment definitions from Biggs that we would like to highlight: convergent and divergent assessment. Convergent assessment is the process of solving problems that have a particular, unique answer. Biggs describes this as a closed system – an analogy to open and closed questioning – because all solutions converge on the same answer. An information skills example might be setting information retrieval tasks when you have to find 16 references on a topic (no more, no less) doing a search on a single database. Divergent assessment is an open approach where there is no single right answer. Rather than focusing on reaching the correct solution, importance is placed on generating alternatives, perhaps even identifying individual assessments of value, originality etc. We might do this by asking people to research a topic and then present back what they have found, discussing how they went about the search and how they decided what was relevant.

So have we defined assessment? We rather liked Rowntree's 1977 definition, quoted in Ramsden (1992, 184) that assessment is about getting to know our students and the quality of their learning. As teachers we can make choices as to how we design the assessment and the values we place on it, and of course our circumstances will mean that we have different kinds of opportunities for assessment, but fundamentally assessment is essential to the teaching process.

Reasons for assessment

There are several reasons why you would assess. The list below is drawn from a number of sources, particularly EduLib (McNamara and Core, 1998) and Ramsden (1992).

To support learning

The fundamental purpose of assessment is to support and improve the quality of learning. For many learners the curriculum or course content is defined by the assessment. So the important material is assessed and, conversely, what is not assessed must therefore be unimportant. Reflect on your own experience: we usually have a better recall of training we have done or courses we have attended where there was some form of assessment. This might not have been an exam; it may have been by doing a presentation or through using what we learned immediately in the workplace. Nevertheless our learning experience was reinforced and enhanced by the opportunity to reach a level of confidence in using the new knowledge or skills.

To encourage the development of skills and abilities

Different forms of assessment can be used to develop a wide range of skills within learners. As well as the information skills you are teaching you can also help to support social development (by setting group work), independence (though individual working) and a wide range of personal transferable skills through different assessment tasks like projects, portfolios, problem-based learning or self-assessment. This can be particularly rewarding if you are running a course over a series of weeks or over several hours because you can choose a mixture of practical activities and assessment techniques to provide variety and to enrich your teaching programme.

To give feedback, help and guide learners

Learners can see what they have done correctly and well, and also see what they have done less well. Assessment is a constructive activity supporting the growth and development of learners through the achievement of goals and from feedback. It can even, as Brown and Knight (1994, 38) suggest, provide a model for self-directed learning and hence intellectual autonomy. Most importantly, feedback can change behaviour either immediately or at a later date, or both.

To signal success or failure, give a mark

Assessment measures achievement, although many researchers on assessment query the extent to which it is always valid and reliable. It is also clear that many learners use their performance in assessment to construct their self-identity, certainly in relation to their learning and teaching experiences, and it is not always a positive identity. Learners who are identified as failures will often behave in ways that reinforce that identity. Remember that learners need to know how they are doing and tangible measurement through assessment is valuable. Nevertheless assessment is the only way we can test whether the learning outcomes have been met and the most recognizable way for learners to see that they have achieved what was expected of them.

To motivate learners

We do not want you to get too concerned about arguments about summative and formative assessment, and we should be conscious that some learners are scared and demotivated by assessment. It is usually assumed that assessment is motivating for learners and that it serves a positive purpose in the learning and teaching experience. Remember, however, that assessment does not have to be formal in the sense of learner-produced work and marks and grades. When teaching information skills, assessment will often be made through giving feedback to learners about some practical work they have completed, often within the learning and teaching event itself. You use the assessment to encourage your learners to work through and complete an activity or series of activities, and it helps to form and embed the learning experience.

To find out how effective teaching has been

You will find this particularly important. Just as we have emphasized the importance of the audit process in Chapter 4, assessment is the process of checking whether the learning outcomes have been met. Use assessment to measure learning, diagnose misunderstanding and identify the next stages of development for the teacher and the learners. Ramsden (1992, 186) has a very attractive description of assessment as being about 'understanding the processes and outcomes of student learning, and understanding the students who have done the learning'.

Assessment principles

We now need to turn to an examination of the underlying principles of assessment. Most texts identify similar criteria, the following list largely follows the EduLib portfolio (McNamara and Core, 1998, 200) with our own commentary.

Validity

Assessment must match what the programme is trying to achieve and the culture it is trying to create and, most importantly, it must test the learning outcomes that you have set. Contemporary writers value naturalistic assessment methods that fit into teaching, so that assessment becomes an extension of learning and teaching, rather than a strange and scary activity.

Reliability

You should try to ensure that the same results come from the assessment even if it is used by different assessors or over a longer period of time. You should try to do this in two ways. First of all you need to think about the teaching inputs, and in particular whether they are going to be consistent across different sessions – we will explore this idea in Chapter 9 on developing a teaching team. Secondly, you need to think about the learner outputs and in particular the way you are making assessment decisions. For example we have found it is helpful to mark the student assignments you checked first a second time, just in case your grading decisions have shifted.

Efficiency

Good assessment makes the best use of learner and teacher time. Do not spend time thinking of excellent forms of assessment if they will take up too much time for either the learners to complete or for you to design and mark.

Fairness

Check whether your assessment is fair, for example to learners who are dyslexic, who come from different cultures or have differing life experiences. Using a mixture of forms of assessment and more than one medium to communicate your purpose are two of the ways you can work to ensure fairness.

Value

Set assessments that the learners will value. This works in two ways. In the first place, link the assessment to your teaching. You might refer to the assessment when you are teaching the group and show how what they are learning will relate to the assessment they are required to do. Secondly, you should make the assessment relevant and valuable to learners. Ensure that the assessment tests knowledge or skills that your learners need to know – this is desirable but not always achievable, because of the vagaries of timing especially in education. Equally, think about setting forms of assessment that are meaningful to your learners. In a literature searching workshop this might mean that your assessment is for learners to find information relevant to their projects, or using business-specific examples in the workplace.

Assessment in practice

Traditional assessment over-emphasized memorization and specific forms of assessment, in particular examinations. Thus factual knowledge, speed of writing and thinking, luck and the ability to work under pressure were rewarded. It was assumed that this was appropriate since these same qualities would be most useful in work and life. There was perhaps some truth in this when higher level education trained people for the professions, particularly medicine, law and the civil service. As society and educational values have changed we are now more conscious of the need to recognize and reward attainment in more diverse ways, and place greater emphasis on feedback and structured learning opportunities.

Librarians and information professionals often get caught up in assessment because they believe that assessment brings power and control over learners and enhances our status. This is particularly true in educational environments when there is endless debate about the role of librarians as teachers. The argument runs that librarians can only have recognition for their role in teaching and supporting learning if they are involved in summative assessment, since assessment underpins the educational system. Your authors are less convinced by this argument and we have found that some of our most effective teaching took place when we were not directly responsible for formal assessment. Even when we have assessed assignments, it may be that our learners still see the assignment as being of marginal importance since it is not related to their main purpose or subject of study.

As the tutor your role in assessment should be to empower and support learners using formative approaches. It is your responsibility to set or agree tasks and assessment criteria that are meaningful to the learners and professionally valid. You must give full feedback, as rapidly as possible, and identify points for development with your learners. Rather than seeing assessment as a means to power, view it as a force for education and do your best to foster intrinsic motivation by being interesting and enthusiastic at every stage of the learning and teaching process.

Planning assessment

The kind of assessment you will conduct will depend on your context. You have more scope for richer and varied assessment strategies when you are running a course over a period of time than if you are organizing a short session. You need to think about your organizational culture and expectations when assessing. It can be more comfortable for you and for your learners to have something that fits existing systems and, if time is short, we would probably recommend that you do this. We are not advocating conservatism for fear of rocking the boat: there is much merit in making groups experience different forms of assessment, but to get them ready for it takes time, and if you only have an hour in total it probably is not enough! We suggest that it can be valuable to reflect the needs, language and culture of your learner community in designing assessment: mimic real work scenarios when assessing workplace learning, for example.

Remember assessment is time-consuming both for you as the tutor and for the learners. Think when you are drawing up your teaching programme how much time you need to allow for assessment either within the session or outside. More complex forms of assessment take longer to set up. If you decide to use self or peer assessment, you will need to spend a fair part of you teaching time explaining how to do it (although you will have to do less at the end of the teaching since the assessment work will be done by others). Much will depend on whether your learners will get some kind of credit from completing a course and whether you can mark work for learners.

Brown and Knight (1994, 39) provide a very helpful description of what makes an effective assessment. They suggest that tasks should:

- enable full feedback
- have criteria for successful completion available
- direct learners' attention to the importance of drawing upon earlier experiences of this sort of activity or to previous encounters with this sort of subject matter, situation or problem
- have review points built in to pause or reflect
- be achievable, in particular be linked to existing or emerging competences
- reflect the goals of the curriculum.

Assessment criteria must follow the aims, objectives and learning outcomes and it is good practice to avoid any new content and dropping surprises onto your learners at this later stage in the learning and teaching process.

Sometimes you can have a very creative or robust idea for assessment – both its form and criteria – but you must check and see that what you have prepared meets the assessment principles we have already discussed. You will need to think about your assessment criteria. Decide whether you are going to give out marks or scores. You could assess purely through feedback – 'That's good, but try this way and see if it's better' – or you can give marks (for example from a quiz), or award pass and fail categories or grades. In the case studies at the end of this chapter we will explore in more detail how you can arrive at assessment criteria and marking schemes. As a check see whether your assessment answers these questions to your satisfaction:

- What do we want to measure?
- Is this the best format to do this?
- Is what we are measuring important?

While you are planning your assessment think about how you will give feedback to your learners. Is your assessment going to require written feedback in the form of written comments, feedback sheets or model answers? Or are you going to rely on individual or whole group oral feedback?

Forms of assessment

So far we have discussed principles and the general application of assessment. We now need to consider what kinds of assessment we will use. The list below is an example only. It is by no means comprehensive and exactly how you will apply the various forms depends on your choice and your circumstances.

The different forms of assessment can be used for either summative, formative or a hybrid assessment. Some approaches are more convention-ally applied for summative purposes (like examinations) but they are also used formatively (mock examinations). There are no fixed rules for what kind of assessment must be used. Remember as well that assessment can take place during learning and teaching events (even within a lecture), within a course (series of learning events you have organized) or outside your teaching and your immediate control.

Bibliographies

Compiling bibliographies is one of the most immediately appealing assessment approaches. You ask your learners to construct a bibliography on an assigned or self-selected topic. The bibliography can vary in complexity from a simple list of books and other sources to a long, annotated, critical bibliography.

Computer-aided learning

This is one of the best-known online learning activities, often taking the form of an online tutorial with a series of activities. Achievement is tested at the end by a quiz or through the construction of a tutorial where you must complete one stage before moving onto the next.

Contribution or attendance

Checking attendance is a minimalist approach, but one that can work well in online environments. In order to pass learners must demonstrate that they attend teaching events.

Case studies

A very effective approach with people in the workplace and with students in professional or vocational disciplines is to ask them to create case studies. Learners are asked to solve a problem that involves using a range of information skills. Business students might be asked to research a company or a market, lawyers to solve a legal problem, health or social workers to research a topic in order to advise a patient or client.

Diaries and logbooks

If you are seeking to develop your learners' personal transferable (also called key) skills, you might ask them to keep a log of their literature searching activities or their experience during fieldwork. This kind of approach is very good at developing reflective practice and can also help with time management and personal organization.

Discussions

Participation in discussion is an excellent way of getting your learners to share their views and opinions. This method is sometimes used in online learning, when the discussion may either be synchronous (in real time) or asynchronous (like e-mail). Participants are assessed for their contribution. It is common in online learning to require your learners to make a minimum number of postings. As a tutor you will often need to structure the discussion, perhaps by posing questions to start the debate, moderate the discussion or assigning different roles in the discussion forum.

Essays

Essays usually comprise a formal discussion, following accepted academic conventions, of a question that you have asked. An essay normally has a sustained argument and uses evidence from published sources to develop its thesis. Assessment criteria for an essay may include an element for the use of sources and accuracy of referencing.

Group work

There are many kinds of group work, and we discuss some of these in Chapter 6. You may decide that your learners will get the best from the learning and teaching experience in a group, and you set a task that they need to work together to achieve. This can be in face-to-face teaching by asking them to go and research something together, do a presentation, and so on, or online when you set a group task or look at group discussions. Remember when you are assessing group work that you can include components for individual contribution and incorporate self and peer assessment, which will encourage your learners to value the process and reflect on their own performance.

Integrate into other work

If you do not have any direct input into formal assessment, see if you can persuade academic staff (in academic environments) to include a component reviewing learners' understanding of information skills into another assessment.

Mindmaps

Mindmaps can be a creative way of getting your learners to show what they understand about a problem and to test their thinking skills. Ask them to devise a mindmap on a topic you have assigned or they have selected.

Multiple choice questionnaires

There is a considerable literature discussing the validity of quantitative approaches to assessment. Multiple choice is often a test of recall and is often criticized. However, if questions are asked in the right way multiple choice can be used to test understanding as well as knowledge. Multiple choice questionnaires are a very good and easy way of assessing online since programs like Questionmark Perception are readily available, and are often integrated into virtual learning environments.

Multi-stage assignments

Multi-stage assignments comprise a combination of several of the forms of assessment we have already described. Often this can be the fairest form of assessment since it tests a range of skills and abilities; but it is time-consuming.

Portfolios

Asking learners to compile a portfolio is a popular form of competence-based assessment. Learners compile a portfolio of the work they have done either following a strict rubric from the teacher or one of their own devising. Our experiences of portfolio-based assessment are mixed. They can be very empowering, with learners who are wary of more formal approaches enjoying gathering and presenting evidence and experienced learners able to present evidence from their work rather than creating new material for the sake of it. At other times learners report that the process of compiling portfolios is unnecessarily bureaucratic, becoming more of an exercise in ticking boxes than allowing scope for individual learning and development.

Poster displays

Poster displays are similar to presentations. Learners produce posters to highlight their learning. You might ask them to summarize sources on a topic or what they have found out about a topic. This will test presentation and design skills as well as information retrieval. People who may not enjoy speaking in front of others will prefer this kind of assessment to a presentation, yet you may find you have similar learning outcomes.

Practical assessment

There are many kinds of practical assessment but by this general description we mean the 'Go and do something' variety, perhaps a hands-on session using the internet, searching databases and so on. Your assessment would normally be formative, advising learners on what they are doing well, and offering suggestions for what else they might do. Practicals may include group work or be individual.

Presentations

Presentations can be individual or group-based. The standard format for assessment through presentation is for your learners to report back about something they have done. This might be a case study but the preceding task can cover a diverse range of activities. Presentations are very good at team-building, can engage the interest of your learners and provide opportunities for summative and formative assessment.

Projects

By projects we mean longer pieces of work. Learners are given a project to complete and a certain length of time to work on it. The exact nature of the project can be set by the tutor, by the learners or together. Project-based learning can be a good way of integrating many different skills and learning outcomes. This is another activity that can be done by a group or individuals.

Publishing

Publishing tests more than the simple retrieval of information, because learners are asked to produce their own materials. This might be a very helpful form of assessment if your learning outcomes include ICT as well as information skills.

Questioning

Questioning can be used to test knowledge and understanding and is particularly effective in informal situations.

Quizzes

Quizzes are a tried and tested format, which can be applied in a variety of ways. You might use a quiz to test recall or as a way of getting learners to use specific information sources. Remember to include an opportunity for feedback, either by getting learners to mark their own work (having been given the solutions), passing the quiz onto others or by providing an answer sheet. Quizzes can be individual or group activities.

Reading cards and reviews

Reading cards test how well learners can summarize the content of what they have read and found and develop critical and evaluative skills. This can be very effective in getting learners to appreciate the informational and academic content of material, be it web pages or journal articles. You might need to establish some criteria or guidelines for how to do the task, otherwise in our experience people will often base their judgements on aesthetic considerations rather than content. A more sophisticated example of this approach is the critical appraisal described in the second case study in Chapter 5.

Reflective essays

Reflective essays are a variation of the academic essay: learners are asked to produce a personal account of the course, their knowledge or skills development. This method is often used in online and open learning to integrate human experience into academic delivery.

Reports

Quite different from essays, reports are structured accounts of a topic. Reports are effective simulations of work practice and can be good assessment formats for an analysis of a case study. You will need to advise your learners about the appropriate format for a report and remember to include report-writing as an intended learning outcome.

Tests

Tests take many forms and in this context should be time-constrained. It might be completing a multiple-choice questionnaire, a CAL package or writing an essay under exam conditions. Online learning offers a lot of opportunities for online assessment, but make sure you are testing what should be tested rather than what is easy to test.

Tutoring others

It is a truism that you only really understand a subject when you teach it. Getting your learners to tutor each other can be an effective way of developing group identity and in encouraging confidence in your learners. Your learners can assess each other's performance as tutors or assess their own contribution.

Worksheets

Worksheets are often used in open and distance learning, but can be used in face-to-face workshops as well. Assessment may take place on completion of the worksheet either simply by reaching the end (formative) or handing in for marking (summative).

Who does the assessment?

We have already alluded to the problem faced by many of us teaching information skills – that we do not have control over summative assessment. As we have already suggested, you should try to build opportunities for formative assessment into all your practical teaching, and remember that this does not always have to be teacher-led. There are convincing arguments for the value of peer and self-assessment and the interactive teaching approaches that work best with information skills delivery are very complementary to learner-led assessment.

Self-assessment is said to develop judgement in learners, giving them greater ownership of the assessment process, and can be particularly effective at encouraging reflection and developing other transferable skills. Evidence suggests that self-assessment is often very accurate (Brown and Knight, 1994, 52). It can be used easily in informal assessment – 'How do you think you got on?' – and is very useful for evaluation activities. Yet learners may be resistant to self-assessment because they do not see it as their role to undertake such assessment or they lack confidence.

Peer assessment is also a possibility. We have identified some potential approaches to peer assessment in the description above; peer assessment has been used to mark reports (against tutor-defined assessment criteria), presentations, group work, worksheets and more.

The main drawback of using self and peer assessment is that it can be time-consuming. You need to prepare your learners for this; it is often best to use this method of assessment when you are running a course over a period of time. But we do not wish to be too prescriptive: choose your assessment approach depending on your intended learning outcomes, the assessment principles we have outlined and what you know about your learners. It is, as ever, up to you!

How to mark

If you are doing the assessment, the rules are simple. Look at the intended learning outcomes and the assessment criteria you have devised, then look at the learners' work. Does it meet the standards and to what extent?

Of course, in practice you might want to check your assessment standards. When we are marking we will revisit the work that we looked at first just to check that we have applied our criteria consistently, and check through a sample at the end as well. You also need to be conscious of your personal bias. Do particular solecisms make you angry? Are there potential difficulties because of the diversity of your group of learners? Baume and Baume (1996) have produced a very clear and simple guide to assessment and marking, and we would not wish to repeat what is presented so clearly and authoritatively there, but some of their key points are:

- Draw up a marking scheme, which can be detailed or in outline only.
- Decide within your marking scheme whether you are looking for right and wrong answers (the product) or if you are going to reward the process as well.
- Give your learners scope to present their own material, findings or ideas.
- Ask someone else to check over your marking scheme.
- When you mark check your consistency and, if possible, ask someone else to double mark your assessment decisions. This helps to establish reliability and fairness.
- Practise marking with model assignments.

Giving feedback

The final part of the assessment process is giving feedback to learners. You have a number of options about how you provide your feedback.

Oral feedback

You can give oral feedback to individuals or to a whole group as part of a formal or informal process. Much of the time we give oral feedback to our learners by encouraging them if they have done well or suggesting how they can improve what they are doing. Feedback to a group can be a very effective way of closing an interactive teaching session. You might choose to draw out an example from one member of your class and illustrate to the group how to solve the problem.

Written feedback

Written feedback takes a variety of forms. You might write comments on individual assignments, highlighting good practice and identifying areas for further development. This is personalized and is often valued by learners. Alternatively, if you are working with large numbers you might develop a standardized feedback sheet where you can check boxes for generic comments or mark along a scale (from well researched to poorly researched) and still have space for individual comments. This can save a lot of time and be an effective way of showing the extent to which learning outcomes have been met. You can see this approach with some online learning systems, where for example completion of a multiple choice questionnaire results in a personalized feedback report. You can try this yourself if you find one of the many personality-testing or careers guidance sites on the web. They seem personalized, but responses are actually generated from answer banks.

Another form of written feedback is the model answer or tutor's commentary, which is often used in online learning when the tutor summarizes the work of a group and provides an evaluative commentary. This can be particularly useful when you are doing a post-experience course, when learners learn almost as much from each other as from the tutor. The teacher is transformed into a facilitator or moderator.

Feedback in online learning

Online learning can provide very rich experiences of feedback because it can be such an interactive medium. Because so much of the teacher and learning experience can be recorded through online discussions, records of the conversations and interactions become part of the learning medium and feedback is tied more closely into the whole of the learning experience. In face-to-face teaching the more sequential and linear approach of teaching will often mean that feedback happens at the end of the learning event, and your learners may not always take away as much as you may wish.

Peer and group feedback

Peer and group feedback can be given orally or be written: the same conventions apply.

The language of feedback

Be careful about the language you use when giving feedback. We always remember criticisms more keenly than positive comments, so consider how to make your point, especially if it is critical. It is often a good idea to use the 'praise sandwich' approach: start positive, then give any criticisms and end with positive comments. Try not to use words like failed, useless, stupid, error, mistaken or foolish. Instead be constructive and include suggestions for improvement. Link all your feedback to the learning outcomes and assessment criteria and try to make it specific so your learners can act on it. You might also think about how to encourage and help learners to give each other feedback and to reflect on their own work.

Final thoughts: improving practice

Assessment of some sort is essential to teaching. Try to build some form of formative assessment into every session and remember that it is less about testing and sorting out learners than reinforcing and supporting your goals in learning and teaching.

Assessment is the final element of the learning process and a way of motivating and encouraging your learners. It is also a valuable way of finding out about your learners and improving your own practice.

Teaching information skills is usually about processes as well as outcomes so try to set tasks that mimic realistic problems and reward achievement in the process as well as the product. You can broaden your own experiences and those of your learners by using a variety of forms of assessment. Don't be scared to experiment, and try to involve learners in assessment activities, either by giving them choice over what they do and what goals they set or through using self and peer assessment.

Reflect back to the learning outcomes. It is appealing to test what can be measured easily rather than what is important. Ramsden's (1992, 212) advice is very sound: use validity (is it important) before reliability (is it consistent) as your critical test. You will find that much of the time this means that you will play a very active role in assessment, so remember to leave sufficient time for it and give plenty of feedback.

Case study 13   Good practice in assessment

Jenny is a subject specialist librarian working at a university in England. She teaches on a mandatory first-year academic skills module, which is taken by more than 300 students in the faculty. The module is well established, having run in its present form for four years and in previous versions for some ten years in total.

The purpose of the module is to prepare students for university life, so that by the end of it they will be confident and competent learners in higher education. It covers a mixture of hard and soft study and research skills, ranging from advanced IT (particularly web page design, use of presentation software and spreadsheets) to academic writing, report writing, group work and presentation skills, as well as information literacy, which is Jenny's specialist area.

Students attend two weekly seminars during the course of the semester and within each session there is a focus on active learning using a number of different approaches, including worksheets, group work, computer-based learning packages and student presentations. Several different forms of assessment are used with some formative (and non-grade-bearing assessment) taking place within the sessions. The main assessment for the module is by portfolio and each week students must complete a reflective log and list their relevant activities for the assessment. There are two other assessments: an individual subject bibliography and a group presentation on academic practice. Attendance is compulsory for at least 80% of the sessions and students fail the module if they are not present.

Jenny was involved in the design of the whole module but only teaches the four-week information literacy strand. She does all the assessment for the subject bibliography and is particularly proud of the work that she has done in creating a well designed assessment tool.

Jenny's assignment requires the students to demonstrate that they are able to identify and map keywords on an assigned topic, they must then list a small number of references, correctly cited, and state which secondary sources they used to obtain the necessary information. Finally, they must also indicate whether those items are available in the library. Because of the increase in collusion or, in the worst cases, deliberate plagiarism, students are given their research topics from a list drawn up by Jenny. Since the faculty is multidisciplinary, the topics tend to be very general rather than linked in to any particular subject.

Jenny worked out a detailed marking scheme, which allocates marks for use of keywords, accuracy of citation, relevance and currency of references, appropriate selection of sources and a small element for presentation. She also devised very clear standardized feedback sheets and also some model answers to distribute with her feedback. Even better, each year student results have been scattered across all grades in a normal distribution, so it looks as if the assignment is a good test of performance.

Students seem to be quite happy in the classes, which are run by some charismatic and able teaching staff. Many struggle with understanding the requirements of the bibliography assignment in particular, especially in recognizing that they just need to find the material rather than read and report on it. The very detailed assessment criteria can also cause some confusion because students often need clarification about what is meant by correct referencing and how relevance will be assessed.

On the other hand a minority of students give the module very poor evaluations, and the failure rate is higher than average in the faculty. A lot of students fail through non-attendance and this has been commented on by an external examiner. Support among the other teaching staff is waning since they are concerned about the negative effect that the module appears to have on the learning experience of some of their students. A few teaching staff are openly voicing an opinion that the module doesn't deliver the intended learning outcomes because students still have to be taught how to follow referencing and essay writing conventions in specific subject areas, and need help with literature searching. Even worse, there are rumours that the module is only running to prevent redundancies.

Questions

1. What would you do about the module?
2. Using the five principles of assessment outlined above (validity, reliability, efficiency, fairness, value) how would you evaluate Jenny's assessment practice?

Discussion

The argument we will make in this case study is perhaps one of our most controversial, since both your authors are neutral about the value of generic skills modules like this one. Such modules are common in the UK, and one of us has even taught on several of them. You are welcome to disagree with us, and we acknowledge that a lot of people will.

In devising this module, the course team appears to have thought very carefully about how to develop the skills of first-year undergraduates. Jenny and her colleagues have devised a module that tries to create a rich learning experience, using a wide array of delivery methods, and a mixture of forms of assessment. They have used design principles that reflect an understanding of excellent practice in learning, teaching and assessment, and we are sure that any review of the module would show that it met its aims and objectives very well.

Our fundamental query is whether the same intended learning outcomes of skills development can be integrated into the teaching of the academic disciplines that the students are studying for their degrees. The ability to research a topic and present your findings effectively are required in every area of study, so why should the skills be separated from the subject? In our experience the most effective learning takes place within a subject context, and abstract assignments like Jenny's, although valid, reliable, efficient and fair, lack value.

Jenny's assignment is not even really testing information literacy *per se*, but information retrieval and presentation. It would be interesting to ask the students whether they reused the skills required for this assignment when they did coursework in their own subjects. How effectively does researching a brief bibliography prepare a learner for the task of reading and analysing that information, of developing the kinds of critical appraisal skills that Isabel teaches in the NHS (see Case study 8)? This is particularly the case when learners research generic topics, so they cannot choose something relevant or interesting to them.

Even within the module, despite the diversity of assessment instruments, are all possible options being explored? If a decision is made to keep the module, are there opportunities to develop self and peer-led approaches to assessment? Getting the students to set the agenda for their learning, and perhaps providing increased opportunities for subject contextualization, might help to make the module more relevant in the classroom and to underpin the subject areas that are currently less-well supported.

Case study 14   Informal assessment with a reading group

Nicola Berry is a community librarian working for a public library service. As well as managing several libraries she is responsible for reader development, working with other agencies and bookshops to promote reading within the community. Addicted to books, reader development is the part of her job that helped her decide to work in public libraries and from which she derives the greatest personal satisfaction.

Nicola runs a weekly reading group every Thursday afternoon in one of her libraries. Participants are mainly women, mostly retired, who enjoy the social elements of the book group at least as much as the literary parts. In fact, Nicola's experience after one of her early reading groups led her to reassess how to structure the meetings and to identify ways of building in assessment as a way of ensuring participation and the exchange of ideas.

Nicola began to have some difficulties not long after Eva started to turn up regularly for the meetings. She was an elderly lady of indeterminate age, living on her own in a flat. Eva had traces of an Eastern European accent, although she had lived in this English town for over 40 years, and when she got over-excited (which was often) her accent got even stronger and strange phrases started to creep in, as if she was translating from her first language. She was a woman of endless energy and enthusiasm and had been a tireless campaigner for many local causes, ranging from the construction of bus shelters to tree planting, and she was the leading light of one of the local political parties and of the conservation society. She was rather opinionated and extremely talkative.

Eva loved the meetings. Every meeting she brought along some beautiful home-baked cakes or pastries and the tea break became the focal point of the meeting. In fact sometimes the tea break seemed to take up the whole of the meeting, especially when someone (usually Eva) found an opportunity to divert the conversation from the book they were reading onto personal reminiscences of the war or their childhood or other memories of the past. Although enjoyable social meetings, these events were not exactly operating as a book group.

Question

1. What advice would you give to Nicola?

Discussion

Nicola decided to take matters into her own hands and change the way the group was operating, using informal assessment as the key to change. She did two quite simple things to respond to the rather diverted and distracted book group. She decided to concentrate on books and themes that would be more directly interesting to the group's members, in particular stories about World War 2 and its aftermath.

The second thing she did was to change the way that she organized and ran the session, building in assessment through careful planning. Nicola had chanced across a helpful book in one of her branches. The text was on how to manage successful learning and was written by Robyn Peterson (1992). In particular Nicola thought a lot about the chapter on using questions to help learning and followed its suggestions closely.

First Nicola made sure that the room was laid out in the way that she wanted, with chairs arranged in a semicircle. She tried to organize the seating so that Eva was sometimes sitting on the edges of the group from where it was just a little bit harder to take over. Nicola also made sure that she herself was sitting in a position where she was clearly in charge – in front, at a slight distance from the other book group members.

The next advice that Nicola took was in planning the way she would use questions constructively within the session, both to structure the learning and to test understanding. She reckoned that using this format might get other people to participate more fully and perhaps get Eva to quieten down a bit. Nicola was able to use the skills she had already acquired from working at an enquiry desk and in staff management, recruitment, selection and review to determine the kinds of questions she would ask.

Nicola decided to start by asking a simple and clear question, directing it to one named member of the group. Depending on the answer, she might ask the same question of another member of the group or move on to another question. By developing a script and with clearer planning she was able to orchestrate the meeting, using a variety of questioning and listening skills to develop discussion and debate. She found that she still needed to include Eva, but often asked her closed questions with less opportunity for Eva to talk for hours.

The strategy seemed to work. Other participants started to join in discussions almost as much as Eva, and the tea break certainly seemed to take up less time than it had previously. More importantly, the discussions seemed to be more wide-ranging than they had before, even when people started to bring in their personal experiences. When Nicola stepped back to reflect on the group she recognized that you could never make this kind of voluntary activity work perfectly, but she realized that by better planning and using questioning for informal assessment it was certainly more effective as an event than it had been before. And she now felt that most of the meetings' content was based on reflection, discussion and review of the current book they were all reading, rather than being a social circle.

8 Feedback and evaluation

This chapter looks at how you can collect, interpret and use feedback from a variety of sources to amend, strengthen and improve your teaching. We also consider briefly how it might be possible to measure the impact of information skills training.

Reflecting on the effectiveness of your teaching process should be a natural part of your work and structured feedback should only aid this reflection. However, it is often viewed as a chore, something to be done at set times or, worse still, collected whenever you deliver a teaching session. Feedback, like any form of assessment, is liable to make us feel anxious and defensive and hence unlikely to adopt the open mindset that is a keystone of the reflective process. Ramsden (1992, 217) argues that 'Evaluation is a means to understanding the effects of our teaching on students' learning' and without this understanding we cannot hope to improve the quality and effectiveness of our teaching.

Feedback

We will look at feedback from four sources:

* ourselves
* our learners
* our peers
* origins outside the actual teaching process.

However, before examining the sources and methodologies available to us we should explore the rationale for seeking feedback at all.

Why seek feedback?

Obtaining, analysing and reflecting on feedback can be a very time-consuming process so it is important that you keep in mind its primary aim: to improve your teaching and hence the learning experience. In order to achieve this aim you should have some control over feedback mechanisms and you need to see the feedback exercise as a constructive process because otherwise it is unlikely that anything positive will come out it. This element of control is often difficult to put into practice. Feedback is sometimes seen as something that is done to teachers instead of done by them (Ramsden, 1992). We are often tied into existing systems, using methods designed and administered by someone else. A bureaucratic concentration on performance management targets for your unit or department can reduce your feedback to a statistical exercise drained of all worth. Using questionnaires designed centrally and often reused every year can provide data proving that teaching and quality management targets are being met but will, by pooling results, reduce the impact on individual teaching methods and seldom address the actual concerns of the learners.

Before exploring feedback in more detail, we should perhaps define what we mean by it. Feedback from learners may be available in a number of different ways, and we will discuss them in more detail below. There are two fundamental types of feedback:

- *qualitative*, in the form of written judgements, impressions, opinions
- *quantitative*, scores and ratings in response to questions.

Both qualitative and quantitative feedback can be analysed and used to construct hard and soft evaluations, but the two forms often reflect a difference in approach. Qualitative approaches are often used to explore how values and opinions were shifted. Open-ended questions are used in order to seek some form of continuing dialogue. Quantitative approaches are better for measuring satisfaction since they provide more concrete evaluations.

Key issues about feedback

Timing

You should consider collecting feedback only when you have a question or questions to ask, when you are open to comments from your learners and, most importantly, when you can do something about the issues that they raise. It is tempting, once you have an effective mechanism, to ask for feedback from your learners at every opportunity. This is rarely a good idea. Ask for feedback when you are new to the group, when the content is new to learners or to you, when you are using new technology to deliver the learning or when your learning strategies are new. Evaluate the learning process, the environment, the learning materials, and your performance if you wish. Explore the wider learning context, asking how the learning is fitting into the wider picture, or about the appropriateness of your material to these particular learners. In each case ask when it is relevant to you and/or to the learners and be in a position to act on the feedback that you receive. Asking whether the course or session is worth pursuing is not a good idea if you have no choice but to continue it, but asking for feedback on specific elements of it can enable you to amend your teaching to rescue a failing situation.

Bad habits

New teachers may be anxious to know how they are performing and this desire may override concerns about the effectiveness of the learning of those they teach (although the performance of the teacher will obviously affect this too). When using feedback to find out about bad habits check whether your group can hear you or whether you have an annoying habit of standing in front of the screen. When you have asked this a few times, and reflected on the answers, you should move the emphasis on to the group's learning and away from your teaching. Everyone likes to know how well they are performing but this wish can easily assume an importance out of proportion to any value it brings to a teacher's performance.

Framing questions

When framing your feedback questions think about whether you want to diagnose a problem or look for solutions to ones that you are already aware of (McNamara and Core, 1998). This will affect both the questions you ask and the way that you approach the answers you that receive. For example, a question like 'name three things that could be improved about the workshop' will enable you to discover any problems learners are having, some of which you may be aware of while others may be new to you. Alternatively a question asking 'how could the workshop have been improved' should elicit concrete suggestions for change from the learners' perspective to add to your reflections on the session.

The type of feedback that you choose to use will depend to a large extent on the sort of data that you want. Decide early whether you want quantitative or qualitative data, or possibly a mix of the two. We will look at examples later in this chapter but your choice should be based on the type of questions that you want to ask and your ability to deal with the responses. Quantitative data can be easily and quickly analysed using appropriate software whereas qualitative data usually requires more time and effort to work through. There has been something of a move away from quantitative surveying towards qualitative, what Parlett and Hamilton (1977) cited in Light and Cox (2001) call 'illuminative evaluation'. This concentrates on what it is like to be a participant, and takes into account cultural, social, institutional and psychological variables. Using quantitative data leads the unpractised analyst towards seeking average ratings and this will often conceal the real concerns of learners. These are more easily expressed by giving them at least the option of expressing some qualitative opinions. We will discuss this point further in the case studies at the end of the chapter.

Perspectives

You should also decide whether you wish feedback to be given from the perspective of the teacher or of the learner. Are you allowing learners to express their own concerns or are you forcing them to answer questions about your agenda? It is possible to address both viewpoints in well designed feedback but it is also easy to slip into a line of questioning that leads the learner away from anything that may be too difficult to deal with. This is particularly true when using centrally designed questionnaires, which may be used for very different groups and situations without the opportunity to customize them in any way.

Timing and delivery of feedback

Once you have decided on the method to be employed consider the timing and delivery of your feedback. Most feedback is collected at the end of a learning experience; we have all been on the receiving end of the 'end of workshop questionnaire' handed out when all we want to do is catch the train. Timing feedback mechanisms at the end of sessions has two major drawbacks: it leaves you with no time to act on the feedback to improve the learning experience of current learners and it diminishes the likelihood that your learners will see any value in the process.

Hounsell, Tait and Day (1997) assert that feedback should be sought before, during, immediately after and a long time after a learning event. Feedback before a learning event is part of the audit process covered in Chapter 4. Asking for feedback during an event will allow you to amend your plan or your delivery methods while there is still time, and this need not be too time-consuming. Asking learners what they think before and during a teaching event will not betray weakness or a lack of preparation but will show that your desire to match the learning methods to their needs is genuine and that it is worth them taking the process seriously. Asking for feedback immediately after a learning experience is useful while the event is still fresh in learners' minds. You might also consider whether to follow it up some time after the event to allow for a more considered reflection on the part of the learners and a chance for them to have seen the value of their learning. In our context the chance to remain in contact with learners for long after our intervention is sometimes limited, but it is worth pursuing this option if possible. Feedback given at the time of a teaching event is coloured by a number of variables, which can give a false picture of the things that you are asking about. Learners may have had a headache, been recently fined by your service desk, found the seats uncomfortable or have any number of other reasons that make them react in a particular way to your input. And the real value of the learning may only be recognized after learners have had the opportunity to practise what they learnt or have undergone some other form of assessment. Leaving a space between the learning event and a follow up to your feedback can allow the bad impressions to fade away and the real learning impact to grow in strength.

It requires careful timing to obtain a decent completion rate of feedback forms. Feedback fatigue can reduce response rates, and the value of the information you obtain. Although most people are happy to be asked for their opinion, asking your learners to fill in yet another questionnaire will not guarantee either their full attention or anything other than a rushed attempt to complete your lovingly crafted effort before heading for the next lesson, bus or café. Timing feedback for the end of the session means that you need to allow time before the scheduled end of the class and convince learners that their completion of the feedback form is more than a selfless act for the benefit of those who follow. Tell your group of any changes made to the session as a result of previous feedback. If you obtain feedback during a teaching session act on any advice as soon as possible, if it is feasible to do so. Using a third party to distribute and collect feedback will sometimes invest it with additional authority which may improve completion rates, but someone standing at the front of a room obviously waiting to collect the feedback forms may exacerbate the tendency of many learners to try to complete the exercise as quickly as possible. The third party needs to be briefed about the context of the request for feedback and sensitive to all parties involved.

Methods of feedback

Self-assessment

We might typify good teachers as always evaluating what they do, seeking to improve their performance and the learning facilitated by their actions. You will almost certainly be placed in a good position to comment on how the teaching went but be careful because you will also probably be your own greatest critic. Remember to balance your reflection with other sources and to look for strengths as well as weaknesses.

An excellent way of obtaining feedback is by observing your learners. Look for non-verbal clues like yawning, chatting and reading e-mails, which show that you have lost the attention of the group. Conversely a group that responds enthusiastically to your teaching methods, which asks questions, engages with the material or is simply attentive is in effect providing favourable feedback. Groups that help one another to perform tasks and take part in brainstorming or other similar activities are giving valuable and positive feedback. Make a note of unsolicited feedback; comments from the group overheard as they leave and learners saying thank you or sending complimentary notes and letters after the workshop are powerful evidence that your teaching has had a positive effect.

There are tools that you can use to aid self-reflection. Consider whether you might like to arrange for your sessions to be videoed and watch them with a structured set of questions. Look for positive elements in your performance but also watch the reactions of the learners. Hounsell, Tait and Day (1997) suggest using a self-assessment questionnaire, which can be completed at the end of a teaching session. The questionnaire should not be long or complicated but must ask you to assess how well you thought you did and to reflect on what you would add, change or omit from the session next time. Used regularly these can build into an excellent body of evidence and offer valuable strategies to improve your teaching.

Learner feedback

Learners are in a unique position to view and comment on their learning and obtaining feedback directly from your learners is probably the most heavily used method of obtaining feedback on teaching but often the least thought through. Carried out mechanically it can quickly become a chore for learners and teacher. Many teachers fear this sort of feedback, worrying that the learners will use it to make personal attacks or ill-considered comments about things that can have no bearing on their learning. Gibbs and Haigh (1984), however, cite evidence that learners will usually want to please their teachers and are generally positive when giving feedback. However, this can mask problems and it is worth treading carefully with learner feedback. Hounsell, Tait and Day (1997) caution that some material is unpopular and difficult and obtaining feedback from learners is not the same as obtaining feedback from consumers. It requires commitment and capability to be a learner, but these qualities are not necessary in consumers.

You will need to overcome the effects of feedback fatigue and other variables that can affect results. For instance, your results might be affected by a poor learning experience from a previous 'library session' or the fact that you have followed a star performer in their previous lesson. The key to effective learner feedback is to make the feedback an active learning experience for learners by involving them fully in the process and by helping them to feel that they have some ownership of the results.

Always tell learners why you are asking them for feedback and what can change because of it. Ask them at the start of the session what they want to get out of it and build this into your feedback. Allow them to influence the feedback agenda as this will help ensure that you are addressing their concerns rather than simply asking them to answer on your terms. Make the feedback useful for them by asking them to reflect on what they have learned and how their learning has been shaped by the teaching session. This will need careful timing and considered explanation. Many learners still expect the teacher to be almost infallible and do not understand why they are being asked to comment on anything other than simple environmental or performance issues. It is worth helping these students to take control of their learning; asking them to reflect like this is a useful way of starting the process.

Make sure that you find some method of reporting on learners' feedback. Post notices, physically or electronically, or pass your reflections on what they have said through a third party if your contact with the learners has ended. This will enhance their perception that they are a full part of the teaching process and increase the chances that they will participate in subsequent feedback exercises.

Questionnaires

Analysing completed questionnaires is probably the most common way of obtaining learner feedback. Questionnaires are quick to administer and evaluate, can be adapted easily to an electronic environment, can be used again and again, deal effectively with the problem of obtaining feedback from large groups and are beloved by managers, who believe them to be cheap and easy ways to manage performance. They are useful in identifying background issues that can subsequently be explored in depth and, by use over a period of time, build up a long-term picture of the effectiveness of teaching.

However, there can be significant problems with questionnaires. Light and Cox (2001) rightly point out that they are 'all too often . . . a simple collection of isolated and ad hoc items'. The common use of tick boxes simply encourages surface reflection as learners try to complete a task as quickly as possible, often in a way that will please the teacher – what Race (1999) calls the 'performing dog' syndrome. He also notes that there is frequently a desire to design questionnaires that will elicit positive feedback, or at least fail to uncover uncomfortable truths, especially when the feedback is pooled. For these reasons think very carefully about the types of question to ask on questionnaires and the ways in which you want them to be answered.

In most cases keep questionnaires anonymous as this will increase the chances of personal feelings being expressed. Try above all to make them look interesting – use attractive fonts and plenty of white space. Try to vary the way that you ask for answers to be delivered but make the questionnaire look quick and simple to complete. Be careful to avoid words that your learners will not necessarily understand. At one of the authors' institutions there is an annual debate about the low scores attached to a question that asks if the students receive timely feedback on their work. Many argue that students do not understand what the designers of the question mean by 'feedback' and assume it to mean a summative mark rather than the helpful and developmental comments that most lecturers offer their students in class and tutorial. Avoid ambiguous or leading statements such as 'Information skills sessions are valuable because . . .' and try to elicit simple responses without clouding matters by including multiple issues within one question, for example 'Does the lecturer use learning technology effectively and respond quickly to student concerns?' Finish by thanking the learners for their valuable feedback.

Questions can be either open or closed. Closed questions usually provide a choice of answers using a scale or a number rating. Boxes might offer a choice between 1 and 4 where 1 is excellent and 4 poor, or ask respondents to mark a line on a continuum, for example:

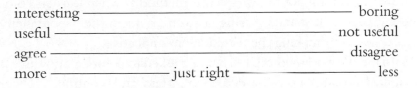

These can be useful options but try to avoid giving a safe middle-ground choice and make your learners give an opinion. One useful way of doing this is to ask learners to prioritize issues, usually by ranking a list of preselected options. This allows you to find out what is important to learners, especially if you offer them a chance to add to the preselected list of choices, and makes it harder for respondents to cluster in the middle ground. It also takes the emphasis away from the teacher's performance, which is often more important to the teacher than to the learner.

Asking open questions is often seen as a simple way to obtain some qualitative feedback using what is essentially a quantitative form. These questions are often unpopular, as a mass of clear white space waiting to be filled in can be intimidating for learners. Some learners also fear that negative comments will be traceable by their handwriting or prose style. Remember that the more open questions you include the longer it will take to process completed feedback. They will also be a hostage to the feelings of the learner at the time and may provoke an outpouring that has little to do with the learning process.

Make your questions unambiguous and focused. Follow up closed questions by asking for comments on the marks they have given and ask for constructive comments, for example 'what changes would you make?' or 'what went well?' as well as 'what went badly?'

Two simple methods given by Race (1999), using open questions, can provide startling results: the 'one-minute' and the 'Post-it' questionnaires.

In the one-minute questionnaire ask a couple of simple questions of the group. These can be written permanently on a board or posted electronically, with attention drawn to them when required. The one-minute questionnaire asks for immediate feedback and should not expect long, considered answers. Snap comments can be very enlightening. Examples of 'one-minute' questions are 'what is the most significant thing you have learned today?' or 'what is uppermost in your mind now?' However, be careful not to overuse this method as when learners come to expect it they will start preparing answers, reducing the spontaneity of their replies, thus making the technique less effective.

With the 'Post-it' method, learners are asked to comment on three pre-distributed Post-it™ notes headed 'stop', 'start' and 'continue'. They are requested to say what teachers should stop doing because it is not working or relevant, what they should start doing in future to improve the learning and what they should continue to do because it is effective. The Post-it notes are then stuck on the door as the learners leave at the end of the session. If Post-it notes are not to hand then the same questions can be used on a single sheet and left on a table. This can provide excellent, constructive feedback although one of the authors once became rather distressed when this form of feedback was used because of the number of adverse comments on his choice of neckwear.

Interviews and discussion groups

Discussion groups or interviews are often useful as a follow-up to questionnaires. Large-scale feedback from questionnaires can be used to identify areas that can then be explored in more detail during a discussion. Of course, this can be achieved through another, smaller-scale, questionnaire but better results are obtained, if time permits, through holding a structured discussion or interview.

Preparation is crucial to the success of these face-to-face methods. The interviewees or group members will sometimes be anxious without the anonymity of the questionnaire so be clear about the procedures and ground rules. These should include an assurance that anything said will not be used for any purpose other than to improve the learning experience.

Methods include:

- *Buzz groups* Individuals write down a key point in answer to a question from the teacher, then combine in pairs, then fours, and so on, to agree the priorities. These are then fed back to the whole group.
- *Rounds* All members of the group report without interruption on issues raised by the teacher or facilitator. This could also be run as a poster tour (see Chapter 6).
- *Nominal group technique* The group give their feelings or answers to an open question; the replies are then collected on a flipchart and ranked in priority order by the group.

These methods are often more considered than a simple brainstorm as they do not rely on instant responses. Individual learners' agendas are more likely to emerge, negatives included, after discussion with their peers. However, these methods are very time-consuming and require more contact with learners than is usual in our experience. Both your authors have used these approaches for feedback after running short courses (of about a week in length) and found them very valuable and constructive exercises for learners and teachers.

Assessment

It could be argued that assessment is one of the best forms of feedback. In testing whether your learning objectives have been achieved (see Chapters 5 and 7) you are also testing the effectiveness of your teaching. However, in most assessments you will have required some commitment and ability from the learners and their performance will reflect this over and above your input. It is worth bearing in mind, though, that an assessment that most fail will generally reflect a poorly planned and executed learning experience.

Representatives

In formal teaching situations within courses there will probably be a student representative who is charged with collecting and reporting student comments and queries about the course. Although the representatives are often not typical of the whole group and will seldom have had time or perhaps inclination to collect feedback from everyone, they do present a different and occasionally insightful source of feedback. This is usually in the context of the course as a whole or the place of your information skills element in the wider learning experience.

It is easy to slip into a defensive mode when facing student representatives but try to avoid this and listen dispassionately. Try to ascertain whether the feedback is from the whole group or represents the representative's own agenda. Feed these comments into your wider picture of feedback.

Use informal channels of feedback from your learners. Unguarded comments can reveal much about their real feelings. Watch how your learners use what they have learned. Are they helping others use the databases you have covered? What type of questions are they asking at enquiry points – do they build on the things that you have covered in training sessions and would now expect them to know? These will all add to the overall picture of feedback.

Peer evaluation

We can learn a lot about teaching from watching others, whether they do well or badly (McNamara and Core, 1998). Those who are obviously skilled can provide us with ideas, techniques and tricks that can improve our practice; those who are less skilled, or simply having a bad day, can show us what not to do. If we add a structure to simply spectating and analyse why things have gone well or badly we have a good tool for evaluating teaching. Sharing our thoughts on our observations turns what is essentially a passive learning experience into something much more dynamic. Although we should be able to reflect on our teaching practice ourselves, having someone to help us will increase the effectiveness of the process.

Peer observation is now a normal part of the academic teaching practice and should be part of our feedback armoury, too. This is not the same as the formal appraisal which is usually part of a management function.

Peer observation should be performed separately from this type of power relationship and both parties should have common agendas and conceptions of teaching for it to work properly.

The EduLib teaching materials (McNamara and Core, 1998, 117) provide a useful list of the requirements of good peer observation. It should:

- *Be supportive and constructive* Although problems should not be ignored any comments should always offer constructive advice on improvement.
- *Be critical and analytic* The feedback should try to analyse why the teaching worked or failed and understand underlying themes, which can be transferred into a broader idea of what teaching is. It should challenge the person observed into justifying rationale and delivery of their teaching.
- *Be explicit to the goals of the learners and the teaching event that you have observed* It should not include other sessions or courses but work with the specific context of the observation.
- *Relate to the teachers' concerns* The observation should be owned by the observed person so it is proper for their concerns to be addressed by the observation. This does not mean that other things cannot be included if relevant but it should address the specific concerns completely.
- *Be discussed and not presented* Good teaching should be a conversation and feedback should mirror this. Although it should not descend into an argument there should be space to discuss both specific feedback and teaching philosophies of the participants.
- *Distinguish facts and opinions* It is important to make it clear when the observer is giving an opinion rather than reporting fact. Opinions can then be accepted or rejected by the observed.
- *Be part of a process* Although it would possibly be counter-productive to go through peer observation regularly it should be seen as part of a feedback process encompassing student and self-evaluation. One or two observations in a calendar year targeted at times when you are experimenting with new methods or teaching a new group would normally be helpful. You should also seek to observe others as part of the feedback process.

- *Be confidential* Unlike formal appraisal and much learner feedback, the results of peer observation should be confidential unless the observed chooses to use it in another context.

The peer observation process should be formal. This will protect both parties from accusations of bias or other misunderstandings. A fairly common practice is to allow 30 minutes before the teaching session for a pre-meeting and another 30 minutes after the end of the observation for a debriefing.

The pre-meeting is a conversation that sets down ground rules for the conduct of the observation and allows the person being observed to identify key areas on which that they wish the observer to concentrate. The observer should also introduce the methodology for capturing the session and agree a time for the feedback to be discussed.

During the observation the observer should make sure that he or she can clearly observe both teacher and learners, but then should attempt to remain inconspicuous. The teacher should usually introduce the observer but thereafter try to ignore him or her.

Feedback should be given as soon after the event as possible, and should follow the standard pattern for any kind of formal feedback or review meeting. The observed person should first be given the chance to comment on the session, if for no other reason than to dispel any feelings of anxiety; then he or she should keep quiet as the observer delivers his or her feedback. When giving feedback the observer should be tactful and sensitive, relating all comments to specific examples. Brutal honesty is not helpful as a lot of damage can be done with careless words. Observers should direct comment to controllable behaviour and deliver the feedback as a 'sandwich', with good practice highlighted at the beginning and end and any constructive, developmental comments acting as the 'filling'. In receiving feedback the teacher should try to remain calm and quiet apart from asking for clarification. It is better to comment only at the end of the feedback and not to argue. An observed person may disagree with the evaluation but little will be gained from venting rage. It is valuable to reflect on feedback later and for observed persons to remember that they own the feedback and can choose how to process and act on it.

Feedback from your peers need not only be delivered as part of a formal peer observation. Post-team teaching discussions can be an excellent way of beginning a dialogue about teaching practice and you should encourage colleagues to engage in conversations about such sessions. We will continue our discussion of this theme in the next chapter.

External sources of feedback

If you are working in education formal teaching as part of a validated award-bearing course will be subject to external feedback as part of the quality systems of your institution or of the wider education system. These include external examiners, quality agencies or professional bodies. All of these can and should be used as part of the overall feedback picture. The formal appraisal systems demanded by most employers also entail the collection of evidence and provide a useful, if stressful, chance to reflect on your teaching.

Evaluation

Once the feedback is collected you need to evaluate it. It is important to treat feedback with respect and try to build a culture where it is received and responded to with positive action. It is wise to watch out for some inherent dangers in this process.

You should try not to dwell on identified weaknesses or get carried away by praise. It may be that you are getting good marks because other teachers are poor, or vice versa. You could be taking the students away from a popular lesson and forcing them into the library when they see little point to the exercise. Low scores are not automatically the fault of bad teaching and good scores do not always signify a good teacher. Milne and Noone (1996, 122) report research that has discovered that those teachers who score highly do not actually often get better results than others and that those students who rate teachers highly may come out of classes knowing less than those with poorly rated teachers. Learner perceptions are not always reliable or helpful with corroborating evidence.

It is tempting to place too much reliance of first impressions of feedback. It is the strongly worded, and often negative, quote that can jump off the page as you flick through the feedback forms. Wait until the feedback is properly analysed before coming to any conclusions, especially with qualitative data. Try to include colleagues in the evaluation process to provide balance. Beware of coming to possibly far-reaching conclusions based on small samples. Plan for criticism; accept what is constructive and ignore the destructive. This is easier written than done!

Use a wide range of feedback tools and process and analyse the results in a systematic and economical way. Triangulate your data with other feedback and with the aims and learning objectives of the session or course to form an holistic impression of your teaching. For example you might explore whether you can triangulate the feedback from the learners with the results of their assessments, performance or behaviour in general. There are so many causes for the variables in evaluations which learners can provide that it can sometimes be interesting to see whether your input has had a positive effect on learning. This might be in the form of changed results in assessment to more simply measured changes such as increased use of databases or library use in general. Many years ago, the impact of the introduction of information skills sessions was made very apparent: library use by those who had attended a session more than doubled!

Always follow up any issues causing concern and do not ignore feedback on the grounds that it is simply learners letting off steam (Hounsell, Tait and Day, 1997). Sort your feedback into issues that need immediate action, those that can be dealt with in the short term, those about which nothing can be done and those things that will need further exploration (Hounsell, Tait and Day, 1997).

Areas for further exploration could be organized by theme, for example improving delivery or by topic, for example lectures, or possibly a mix of the two categories. However you organize the feedback you receive, you should take control of the process and create an action plan. This will ensure that the process becomes truly developmental rather than an exercise in looking backward at past actions and situations. Use the feedback to amend your teaching and fine tune those amendments by targeted future feedback.

Measuring impact

Should you try to measure the impact of your information skills teaching? This is a difficult question to answer. First of all we need to consider what exactly we mean by impact: are we trying to explore changes in attitudes, behaviour, motivation, self-perception, economic benefit, the perceived value and use of libraries and information services or something else? And are we interested in impact at the level of the individual, a group, organization or society?

Framing these questions will help to explain why we are not going to dwell on this topic in any detail. We are asking significant social scientific research questions, open to exploration using perspectives from multiple disciplines and multiple research techniques.

In the UK the Museums, Libraries and Archives Council (MLA) has a vision of making learning accessible in museums, archives and libraries in its *Inspiring Learning for All* (MLA, 2004), which is supported by a toolkit for measuring its learning outcomes (MLA, 2003). Although measuring the impact of libraries on learning is not exactly the same as measuring the impact on teaching, there are some interesting prompts. The toolkit would merit some consideration if you wish to explore this further. Your authors feel, however, that the toolkit has more value as a heuristic device to frame understanding, rather than as a definitive statement.

Equally, within the literature many case studies evaluating the effect of a specific initiative can be found, for example the impact of information skills training. These vary from being evaluations of specific courses, within institutions (Bastable et al., n.d.; Seamans, 2002) or of collaborative research projects (INFORMS and its evaluation report by Anderson, 2003). They use a number of different research methods, ranging from interviews, focus groups, action research (see Barrett and Danks, 2003, for a particularly good example) to citation analyses of essays. Each one tends to be specific rather than general, but we suggest that this may be a more justifiable approach in terms of the rigour and appropriateness of research design. Impact measurement is an open-ended, multi-disciplinary research topic, and we suggest that you frame your research question before exploring the topic further.

Conclusion

Obtaining feedback can be a stressful and time-consuming exercise that is often completed with a sigh of relief and then ignored. This is a waste of a valuable resource. Well planned, timely and clearly presented feedback mechanisms can be a developmental tool for both teacher and learner. Analyse, reflect and act upon your feedback and your teaching, and hence the quality of learning, can only benefit.

Case study 15   'George – don't do that!'

George was a recently qualified librarian who had just started to run a significant number of learning and teaching sessions in his job as a learning librarian within a public library service. When studying on his library and information studies course, he hadn't really expected to do very much teaching; he had deliberately decided not to go into teaching when looking for a graduate career. Instead he wanted to work in reader and community development and had found himself in a job he loved. Rather to his surprise it also provided him with the opportunity to use the teaching skills he had developed when working as a foreign language assistant during his degree and later while teaching English as a foreign language in Japan.

Most of George's work was based around informally supporting and facilitating learning, but he also had some more formal teaching work running training sessions with colleagues and local community workers. Although George was very comfortable planning and delivering sessions, he had little experience of evaluating teaching sessions. It was much easier, he felt, to evaluate whether your teaching was any good if your students had to do some kind of test at the end, and even more so when you really got to know the students during the weeks that you taught the course.

George wasn't very sure how he could overcome this absence of assessment and evaluation. He saw his input into the teaching sessions as part of a developmental process, and he knew that participants were attending largely voluntarily. His managers had not set very clear targets either. He was the first person in this post, and there was a mixture of targets and goals which he needed to meet, only one of which related to his formal training work and that was just a count of number of people who had attended a session.

George decided that he needed to develop a feedback questionnaire to evaluate what people were learning from the session. He did some hunting around and found a few good examples of formal questionnaires that he thought he could use. He liked the idea of developing performance measures and thought he would use a series of questions about his workshops and ask people to rate the value of the sessions on a scale of one to five.

If truth be told, George got rather carried away devising the questionnaire. He ended up with a form that asked 20 questions, ranging from information about respondents' previous knowledge and experience to comments about the process, background information on the participants and evaluative questions about the sessions, covering the management, delivery and content. George was rather pleased with the end product, since it would result in a really comprehensive evaluation and provide plenty of information about what he could do next.

In practice, things didn't work as George had expected. The first time he gave out the questionnaire there was a very low completion rate – only two forms out of 15 were returned. George realized that he had not left enough time for participants to complete the form, nor had he introduced its purpose at the beginning of the session.

The next time he ran a session, George decided to build in some time for participants to complete the questionnaire. He explained its purpose at the beginning and left ten minutes at the end for completion. To his surprise, although the response rate was higher, the feedback was terribly bland. Nearly everyone just circled the middle number and didn't write in additional comments.

Time, George thought, for a rethink.

Questions

1. What do you think George has done wrong?
2. What would you recommend that he do instead?

Discussion

We think George is doing two things wrong. His greater mistake is that he is trying to measure everything in a complicated questionnaire that his participants are finding too difficult to complete. On a more minor note, we think it is usually better to use an even number for rating questions, such as one to four, because it makes it harder for people to choose a neutral score in the middle. We should note that this is really a matter of personal preference (and considerable debate among experts in the field).

George could change what he is doing in a number of ways. First of all he needs to unpack what he actually wants to achieve from the evaluation. We have a number of questions:

1. Is he trying to use the form as an auditing tool? If this is the case, then it might be better to separate out auditing from evaluation.
2. For what does he want to use the feedback about the session? If he wants to build up data about his training he is probably using the right kind of instrument, but this format isn't the best way of identifying what are his current strengths and weaknesses in delivery and content.
3. Is he interested in evaluating the impact of the training? Here he has two options. He can check the immediate response, but perhaps it might be more valuable if he did some kind of follow-up exercise some time later. Often we do not know what the effect of our learning and teaching activities has been until some time after a teaching event. Feedback questionnaires measure immediate responses, and sometimes we do not realize the value of training until some time later.

If George is interested in feedback about the immediate effectiveness of his teaching he should tighten his focus. We think he has two options. The first one is to make the questionnaire shorter and more focused. He should concentrate on aspects of the session that can be changed, rather than all the evaluative and demographic information he was trying to ascertain before. His second option is 'quick and dirty' but it has immediate impact. In the middle of the session George could give out Post-it notes and ask participants to write on one what he should stop doing, on the second what he should start doing and on the third what he should continue to do. As people break up for tea or at some other natural interval they put the Post-its on a wall, by the door or on a flipchart. George can read them during the interval and modify his teaching accordingly.

So George needs to think about the purpose of feedback and evaluation. If you require information about the quality and impact of teaching, then it is important to settle on techniques that will give you information that will help you change what you can do.

Case Study 16 'Lies, damned lies and statistics'

Miriam works in an academic library; staff are very interested in evaluating information skills training and hope to develop some measures and standards for information literacy.

Little progress has been made in the assessment of information literacy, since Miriam and her colleagues are not entirely sure how they can measure its impact within the university experience of the students. At the moment they are investigating the possibility of carrying out an evaluative research project with library colleagues at other institutions, and there are lots of ideas for large-scale longitudinal research projects.

For several years standard forms have been distributed at the end of every formal learning and teaching event. There are two main versions of questionnaire: one for induction and the other for information skills sessions. Both versions contain some questions requiring numerical ratings and others with space for write-in comments. Statements for numerical rating included:

- The session was enjoyable and interesting.
- It covered everything I needed to know.
- It took the right amount of time.
- The session was relevant.

The more open questions asked students what was the most useful element of the session, what was least useful and what recommendations they might make for future sessions.

Forms were collated at course level and then academic school sum-
maries and later headline measures were produced, which were used in
departmental self-assessment reports.

Miriam was rather ambivalent about the forms. She liked getting nice
comments (which happened occasionally) but she found collating all the
data a headache and time-consuming. It was particularly hard to collate
the write-in comments, which were both individualistic and repetitive. At
any level beyond the analysis of a specific session these didn't seem to be
particularly valuable, but at the same time Miriam realized that she needed
some evidence for the value of her input into the academic life of the institution.

Questions

1. Do you think this is an effective evaluation method?
2. Can you think of any alternative approaches to evaluation for Miriam?

Discussion

There are two answers as to whether this is an effective evaluation
method, depending on whether your perspective is that of a teacher or a
manager. As teachers, we might wonder whether the use of these forms
on every occasion actually improves the quality of the teaching. In all honesty Miriam found that most of the time the forms told her what she
already knew. For example, if she had to rush a session when her students
arrived late, there would be comments about lack of time, or if she forgot
to talk about printing costs, that would be mentioned. Sometimes the
comments seemed to be made just for the sake of filling in an empty box,
with people stating that the worst thing about the session had been the
uncomfortable seats or the room temperature.

On the other hand, all university departments were required to develop
and use appropriate performance indicators, and those related to the
effectiveness of the department's role in learning and teaching would only
serve to underpin the importance of their contribution in this area. Even
better, since the data was available over a series of several years it was pos-

sible to draw up annual comparisons and analyse the underlying causes for changes.

But Miriam had some concerns. The number of students who actually attended these sessions was quite small, and she secretly wondered whether they were spending a lot of time measuring something just because they could. It would be far more interesting to triangulate this data against measures of whether students changed the way they found and used information in their academic work, although Miriam wasn't very sure how she should do this.

Your authors are also uncomfortable about the absolute value of this approach. Evaluation and feedback are important but at the level of teaching you must have a purpose and a plan for change. It can be very helpful to evaluate the effectiveness of your teaching, especially when you are working in new territory – with a different group of students, exploring new content or approaches. But relying simply on feedback questionnaires can be limiting. For a start, the only assessment comes from the students. In a university there are often other stakeholders: what do the academics think about the value of the sessions; has it actually changed the behaviour or expectations of your learners in any way?

We are uncertain whether even the numerical ratings are helpful. Most people tend to be more positive in feedback questionnaires than they might be if questioned directly, so you can get a slight bias towards positive responses. There are also doubts about whether the response rate is statistically significant. Attendance is rarely 100% and not all of those present will complete a questionnaire. Thus performance measures are being built on a sample that may be neither valid nor reliable.

From a management perspective it is important to understand what value and impact is coming from library involvement in learning and teaching processes. If questioned directly, the value and contribution of libraries and librarians is generally seen as positive – just like motherhood and apple pie. Evidence is required. But what do we actually understand by that evidence?

We are being pushed in opposite directions. In the UK there is an increasing emphasis on students evaluating their educational experience, and thus pressure on every level of the organization to devise meaningful performance measures and indicators. On the other hand we surely have a professional obligation to be rigorous in the way we approach evaluation and should not rely on such crude data analysis. If we wish to understand learning, these kinds of evaluations are merely a heuristic device, not an end in themselves.

9 Building a teaching team

Rather than focusing this text only within the interaction between teacher and learner we will now consider how you might build a teaching team through skills enhancement, collaboration with others and developing a shared teaching culture. We need to move away from a perception that librarian involvement in teaching and facilitating learning only happens between an individual and a group of learners. Rather, this role is a core part of our work and we need to integrate what can seem a specialist activity into the professional practice of ourselves and colleagues. At the same time, we should not fail to be aware that this process has many other stakeholders, including IT and systems staff, educational technologists, teaching staff and managers, and that in many instances we need to collaborate effectively in order to meet our goals.

There are three discrete themes in this chapter:

- skills development for teaching and learning
- collaboration with other professional and occupational groups
- culture building, in particular through team teaching, peer observation and evaluation.

In truth, each theme is interwoven and mutually supportive: a good skills base will help to develop a teaching-centred culture and probably mean that you are able to build effective working partnerships, but we will explore each in turn.

Skills development for teaching and learning

One of your authors (Powis, 2004) recently published a review on how to develop the academic librarian as a learning facilitator. A striking feature of his research for this chapter was the paucity of published material on development for teaching among library and information professionals. The discussion below is based to some extent on his previous overview, with some additional comments.

Initial training

Very few people are natural teachers, but most people can become competent ones. For some people, competence develops through practice and experience, but consensus in the UK is that expertise can be developed through structured training interventions.

The most problematic stage is what to do at the beginning. Should you be trained how to teach before you do any teaching in earnest, or should the training be available after you have some experience?

Although most library and information professionals will have taken some form of qualifying course, either as an undergraduate or postgraduate, teaching skills do not feature widely on an already crowded LIS curriculum. In part this may be due to a mistaken perception that the learning and teaching role is not generally shared across the profession, but is relevant to academic libraries alone. A more fundamental cause is likely to be the tension between specialist and generic skills in preparation for professional practice. The end result is that most new entrants to the profession have not had any academic development in how to teach or the underpinning theories that can make our input into the learning process most effective.

On teacher training courses and the courses for new university lecturers in the UK, theory and practice run alongside each other. There is some classroom-based learning of theory, which is then put into practice by teaching. New teachers learn how to teach while they are actually teaching. It might be supposed that attending one of these courses, particularly if offered as a short course, would be a suitable option for a new librarian. We agree with this, but in the same way that academics have input from staff in the subject area they work in, it is critical that the differences encountered by librarians are recognized within the classes or assessment design. The fragmentary nature of our interaction with learners and the usual absence of summative assessment can mean that you do not have the kind of experience needed to meet the learning outcomes for some of these courses. EduLib (Core, 1999) and LibLearn (n.d.) are particularly good examples of the application of general teaching courses to a specific LIS context without any compromise in the pedagogic content.

As a minimum, it can be helpful to have some training in presentation skills and approaches to facilitating learning. These courses may be available in-house within your department or organization (though perhaps under slightly different names) and are often run by training organizations. For example, in the UK CILIP runs a short course on teaching skills and techniques that covers all the principles we have reviewed in this text and also provides the opportunity to practise and get feedback in a safe environment.

Mentoring

Another approach to skills development is through mentoring. In mentoring, an experienced colleague, perhaps in the same department, perhaps outside, is identified as a role model and supporter. The mentor helps the protégé or mentee to develop skills and knowledge through feedback, support, advice and guided help in a relationship that is separate from line management.

This can be a very effective developmental approach for three reasons. In the first place, the mentoring relationship is not dependent on line managers, so if you are working on your own or feel professionally isolated, you still have developmental options open to you. It is perfectly possible to identify a mentor outside your own department – a member of academic or human resources staff, or your organization – a colleague in another library or even in a different occupational area. Secondly, the mentoring relationship does not have to be conducted face-to-face but can work by e-mail or telephone calls, making it much easier for a solo professional or a specialist to gain access to the necessary support.

Finally, mentoring can be helpful both at the very beginning of your teaching experience and later on. Acting as a mentor to less experienced colleagues can also provide you with opportunities to reflect on and develop your own practice. Anyone wishing to explore mentoring further should read Clutterbuck (2001).

Qualifications

Despite having some reservations about the value of some formal teaching courses at the outset of your teaching work, we recommend that anyone wishing to develop knowledge, confidence and competence in teaching and supporting learning should consider whether to undertake a course leading to a formal qualification in teaching. In our view this is perhaps most appropriate when you have some experience of teaching, rather than as an introduction to learning and teaching. There are several options.

In UK universities it may be possible to take a postgraduate course in teaching in higher education, be it a certificate, diploma or MA. These were established in most universities and colleges of higher education following the Dearing Report of 1997 (National Committee of Inquiry into Higher Education, 1997). They follow a variety of patterns, with many built around portfolios of practice with reflective essays, although some require students to take taught modules and write essays. Almost all the courses require some peer observation to take place. Sadly, they are not always open to staff in support departments like library and information services.

In the UK many colleges of further education offer qualification courses in post-compulsory learning and teaching, often in the form of a Certificate in Education. These courses are usually offered part-time and are accessible to people working in the wider community rather than just the institution. These are a very valuable option, particularly if you would like to learn face-to-face on a flexible part-time course.

There are still several further possibilities. Many universities and colleges offer other part-time and distance-learning courses on teaching. These may be general teaching qualifications or may cover specific topics, like e-learning or educational management, and can be useful developmental opportunities for the experienced teacher and tutor.

You can identify what is available and suitable for your preferences by searching the internet and looking in course directories.

Continuing personal or professional development

Complacency is a threat to best practice, and it can be all too easy to become complacent as a teacher. You can fall into particular habits or ways of working, continuing with what you know and like and what works well. On one level there is nothing wrong with this approach if what you are using is effective with your groups of learners. On the other hand, if asked, we would probably characterize excellent teachers as being people open to change and willing to be creative and take risks.

Creativity can sometimes be a challenge to those of us working in library and information services. Our professional culture fights against it because of problems of definition and innate tradition. But we do have tremendous opportunities for development through CPD, particularly in the form of projects, courses, conferences and even guided reading.

Within the workplace involvement in projects, either internal or external, can provide many opportunities for development. Projects are test beds for innovation and change, for collaborative working and for the pilot stages of what may become mainstream activity later.

Professional organizations like the UK's University, College and Research Group hold regular meetings on learning and teaching-related topics. These invariably provide the opportunity to find out about and/or exchange best practice and innovation. The meetings also provide plenty of scope for networking and development.

Reading about subjects can be valuable as well. Many of the texts referenced in this book are widely available, but naturally a huge amount of useful information is available on the web. As a starting point in your web searches we would commend the Information Literacy Place (http://dis.shef.ac.uk/literacy/default.htm), which has an extensive bibliography and resource centre on information literacy and the teaching guides at the Learning and Teaching Support Network (LTSN) Generic Centre (www.ltsn.ac.uk/).

This theme links into the emerging topic of evidence-based

librarianship, asking a question, finding and appraising evidence, applying the results and evaluating (Booth and Brice, 2004). This model will suggest ways that you might apply accounts of good practice often found in the literature.

Professional involvement

As well as attending courses and conferences you can join professional groups. You may wish to reflect on where you will get the greatest benefit from involvement. There are two options: an association for library and information professionals (like CILIP in the UK) or a non-LIS organization like the Higher Education Academy (incorporating the Institute for Learning and Teaching in Higher Education, LTSN and HESDA) or the Association for Learning Technology (ALT). Whichever group or groups you choose to join, you will find that member benefits include a professional journal, which may include topical and stimulating articles, as well as conferences and usually mailing lists.

More active professional involvement can be a great benefit as well. Both of the authors of this book are involved in special interest groups (in LIS and elsewhere). Whichever group you choose, you have the opportunity to shape other colleagues' knowledge and understanding, and perhaps even to organize events focused on topics based on your own particular learning needs. You also strengthen and further develop a professional network, which you can draw on in your work, as well as broadening and extending your own skills base through doing new things.

In our experience we found that we gained different types of practical benefits from our various kinds of involvement. Being active within the LIS world provided us with an external network of practitioners working in similar jobs, with whom we could share much of our current experience and talk the same language. Involvement in teaching bodies enhanced our credibility within our organizations and gave us a shared language to speak with academics, educational developers and learning technologists. And both kinds of engagement enhanced the other: we could be credible advocates for library and information professionals outside our professional sector, and promote best practice within the sector through external links.

Reflective practice

The model of a reflective practitioner is very influential in learning and teaching development. Drawn from the writings of Donald Schon (Schon, 1982), the focus is the capacity to reflect on action so as to engage in a process of continuous learning. There are two processes: reflecting in action (while you are doing something) and reflecting on action (after you have done it). We have illustrated how this takes place in many of our case studies, showing ways of modifying what you do during delivery or carrying out a post-event review. Reflective practice is central to our vision of learning and teaching: its processes of iteration and objectivity enable you to focus on the important principles of what you are trying to achieve.

Collaboration

We need to establish formal and informal groups and alliances to deliver effective teaching and learning in information skills. Integration within the life and culture of your organization is critical to the recognition of information literacy and learning support and working with colleagues both inside and outside our own department is now standard practice within organizations. Yet we often start our collaboration full of misconceptions and prejudices. We thought we would begin this section by exploring some of those biases, since we often start collaborative activities unaware of unconscious stereotypes that colour own interaction with colleagues.

Table 9.1 is based on a workshop run by Chris Powis in 2002 (Powis, 2002). Participants were asked to brainstorm perceptions of the main stakeholders in their teaching; comments were to be taken entirely seriously.

If we approach collaborative work with these preconceptions it is hardly surprising that initiatives fail! Julien and Given (2003) found similar results in their study of Canadian librarians' expressed attitudes and perceptions of faculty. These archetypes are preposterous and we need to overcome them to get anywhere. Working with others can be invaluable in teaching and supporting learning. These are just some of the benefits:

Table 9.1 Preconceptions and bias in the teaching team

Who	What librarians think of them	What we think they think of us
Academics or teachers	Pompous, arrogant, out-of-touch, ignorant of what we do, dinosaurs, bureaucratic, possibly helpful, intellectuals	Book stampers, irrelevant, procedure-driven, pedantic, uneducated
Learners	Disorganized, spoilt, wanting to be spoon-fed, unwashed, impatient, unreasonable	Old-fashioned, bossy, helpful, bureaucratic
IT people	Nerds, no good with people, systems-led without any user focus, isolated, unco-operative, secretive	Book stampers meddling in e-things, 'objects of lust'
Educational technologists	Nerds with trendy glasses	Book stampers
Staff developers	Pompous, out-of-touch, preach what they can't practise	Self-important book stampers

- increased motivation of learners and teachers
- improved reflection (through peer observation, team teaching)
- better auditing (using information from your colleagues)
- variation to keep the learners interested
- innovation and breadth of content and delivery by pulling together diverse knowledge, experience and skills
- more reliable environment and infrastructure (IT people actively involved in e-learning will help with technical and design issues, for example)
- greater visibility and political influence.

We enhance our skills base from working with different occupational groups, mixing perhaps the teaching expertise of an academic or staff developer with the programming skills or infrastructure knowledge of an IT person.

It is up to us to be proactive. You will be surprised how willing people are to collaborate with you, and how often our preconceptions and stereotypes fail to live up to the truth. Even more importantly, collaboration can provide a major opportunity to develop your skills, and even to apply them in a different area of work, away from the professional comfort zone of library and information practice.

Culture building

In the previous sections we identified some ways in which individuals can develop their teaching and learning support skills and knowledge and how we can overcome some of the barriers to collaborative activity. We now need to consider how we might develop an organizational culture that is firmly centred on good learning and teaching practice.

Team teaching

One of the best starting points in developing a common culture is in sharing activities through team teaching. There are several rationales for team teaching, ranging from the pragmatic – dealing with large numbers or awkward working hours – to the pedagogic – matching constructivist principles of multiple perspectives and collaboration (Anderson and Speck, 1998) via quality assurance (ensuring consistency of content).

Fox (n.d) identifies several different forms of team teaching:

- *Solo act with back-up* Each individual works singly in the classroom, but is dependent on the team for arrangements outside the learning and teaching event. The extra-classroom arrangements may be collaborative production of materials, regular review meetings, delegation of particular responsibilities or visiting lecturer slots.
- *Solo act with eavesdroppers* Other members of the team sit in or assist with particular classes. This is a particularly effective way of on-the-job training for new staff or involving support staff in teaching and learning support
- *The double bill* Two or more people teach a session together. This can be effective when you are running a long course – like a one-day workshop – or handling a potentially difficult group since you bring variety in delivery and share the direction of the class with another person.
- *Follow your leader* This is an approach often used when teaching very

large modules. One person is owner of the course content but other people are involved in delivery. It can be consistent, but it can also be uncomfortable working with materials prepared by another person.

- *Syndicates* Students are set group tasks and a number of teachers act as consultants or facilitators.
- *Panels* The teaching team arranges for a panel discussion or debate.

For learners team teaching can offer a number of benefits including a wide range of teaching viewpoints, increased expertise, more supportive environments by virtue of a more favourable student–staff ratio and consistency (Anderson and Speck, 1998; Fox, n.d.). There can be particular benefits if the teachers come from different disciplinary backgrounds, for example, librarians and academics or archivists working together.

Team teaching has several benefits for the tutors. It can offer economies of scale or time, since common resources can be prepared and reused, and it is a force for standardization and thus the identification of minimum and optimal standards for delivery. In developmental terms it provides the opportunity for learning by observation and support, so you eavesdrop or support sessions before going solo.

Team teaching is a very useful approach for information skills work. You have opportunities both to practise and develop your own skills in a supportive environment and to have a focus for evaluation and review activities.

Peer observation

Peer observation was discussed in the previous chapter, so we shall not repeat points already made there. Suffice to say that peer observation can be a very effective means of teambuilding, assisting in the development of a teaching identity among a group of peers and providing a focus for individual learning and development. If the peer observation process is owned by the teachers, it can be used as a means of increasing personal responsibility and active involvement in teaching activities. If handled appropriately individual learning points or best practice can be discussed and cascaded within the team without compromising the personal nature of the observation itself.

Building virtual teams

We may find that our team collaboration is less face-to-face than actual. Before exploring how we might overcome these attitudes we need to understand what makes a good team. The literature is wide and varied but common themes emerge. A good team is:

- trained
- committed
- motivated
- innovative
- communicative
- working towards a common goal.

The original concept of teamworking as a management technique came from studies of the Durham coal mines in England and a textiles factory in Ahmedabad in India (Buchanan, 2000). Traditional teams often worked for the same manager or team leader and built their commitment through regular face-to-face interaction and collaborative working. Because of the complexity of organizational structures, separation by distance and/or the increased focus on project working, we increasingly work in virtual teams for some or all of our time. Duarte and Snyder (2001) describe seven types of virtual team:

- *Networked teams* collaborate to achieve a common goal or purpose. Team membership is open-ended and input may be linked to job purpose or particular expertise. An internal staff discussion list where colleagues could ask for help with reference enquiries would be a very simple example of a networked team.
- *Parallel teams* carry out special tasks or assignments usually at the stage of scoping a new idea and making recommendations for change. A group charged with reviewing induction activities and making

recommendations for changes in practice is a good example of a parallel team.

- *Project teams* are responsible for conducting and completing projects. Membership is not always clearly delineated. Responsibility for action is devolved to the team. Were our induction group also responsible for designing and delivering new resources, then it would become a project team.
- *Work or production teams* are groups who regularly work together but may be at a distance of space or time: colleagues who work part-time or at another site for example.
- *Service teams* offer support throughout the day and night; for instance staff working on an enquiry desk. Some library and information services are offering 24/7 enquiry and helpdesk support by partnering other sites or partners across the globe.
- *Management teams* have a distinct identity and seek to achieve corporate goals.
- *Action teams* are usually set up to deal with emergency situations. Membership may be fluid or distinct. The 'all hands to the deck' approach at induction time is perhaps a reasonable example here.

What is unfortunately missing from this private-sector typology is the type of team in which the team leader has no control over some of the team members! The maverick member may be an IT person who is working to different priorities or just a colleague of equivalent status who joins in but at a remove and lacks commitment.

Buckley (2000) offers a simpler typology of teaching teams:

- *Authority-directed teams* are strongly led by one person, usually a manager or director. Roles correspond to your place within the hierarchy.
- *Self-directed teams* meet together for delivery or more commonly development or review activities.
- *Co-ordinated teams* combine elements of the first two; they have a leader but often roles are dependent on input rather than position.

There are ways of building an effective team, virtual or otherwise, which are all essentially techniques to build and develop the qualities we listed above. These include training and teambuilding techniques, leadership, effective and appropriate use of technology. You can apply your experience in motivating learners to managing a team. The same principles apply, particularly working with clear objectives, auditing, defining clear roles for team members and planning are all important.

It can be productive to have some face-to-face meetings, because of the social interaction that this brings. Real meetings can be particularly helpful at the beginning of a project, but they are also valuable as milestones since the social interaction can help to develop a team culture. However, they are not essential, and many successful projects have been conducted only via e-mail, videoconferencing or by phone, but remember that, just as in online learning, as an e-manager you will need to put plenty of work into motivating and structuring your team's activities and actions.

Bringing new members into the team

We have already mentioned some of the ways in which new members of the teaching team can be introduced to their work, but we wish now to apply them to new entrants to the team. New team members must be able to feel valued, supported and able to make a contribution. This can be a difficult balance. It is tempting to assume that younger members of the team may be more innovative and dynamic than their colleagues and will be thrilled to have the opportunity to teach. This can be a misconception: remember that very few new entrants to the profession will have had any formal training in teaching or facilitating learning. Just accept your new people into the team, and treat them as individuals rather than stereotypes. Remember to plan for the induction and training of new team members as becoming a teacher is not just a random activity – this point is reinforced throughout this book.

Management and review activities

Managers can also foster a learning and teaching culture by creating opportunities for planning, evaluation and review and encouraging the formulation of strategic objectives for this area of work. We are not advocating a bureaucratization of learning and teaching activities, but rather a constructive process of establishing a vision and goals for a sphere of activity. Effective management of the range of learning and teaching activities will pull together a disparate range of activities and help to construct a coherent and action-oriented vision of learner engagement.

Managers have a number of options in the strategic development of learning and teaching activities. Depending on the organizational context they may wish to set goals or targets for information skills training or information literacy development. Alternatively project groups or task forces may be set up perhaps with a specific task in mind – at the moment these are often linked to the development of e-learning, information literacy, lifelong learning and social inclusion (McNicol, 2002) or knowledge management (Sippings, 2004).

Developing a shared vision or a strategy for learning and teaching can be a constructive activity. This can start as a position statement or declaration of intent, and thus not only indicate what actions should be taken but also create a shared language with colleagues to focus their own activities.

Members of the teaching team should set aside opportunities for evaluation and review of their activities and preparation and planning for the next time each day. It can often be appealing once you have finished running a course to put all your materials away and move on to the next job: resist this temptation. Sometimes debriefing can be a very valuable form of evaluation, especially if the information gained is relatively current or significant in some way.

Using action learning sets is another way of building a shared culture. Although they are often built around multi-occupational groups (since diversity is one of the strengths of the set), they can be used in a more targeted way around one focus like teaching. Participants bring along a problem or a question they wish to review and members of the set discuss the problem and identify possible solutions. All members of the set have the opportunity to air their problems and be offered possible solutions. Similar in purpose but less problem-focused is an exchange of experience session, in which participants share good practice.

Both action learning sets and informal exchange of experience sessions provide many opportunities for the development of shared understanding between members of a team. Common principles, values and beliefs can be established, which all contribute to the formation of the intangible cultural dimension.

Involvement, action and reflection: building a teaching team

You will build a teaching team in three ways. First of all you need to focus on the development of individual and group knowledge, skills and competences through professional engagement and appropriate training and development. Being an effective teacher does not happen through some kind of charismatic intervention when the circumstances arise, but is a combination of qualities and skills, which can be developed in almost everyone.

Secondly, much of our competence in teaching and facilitating learning is reached by gaining experience of a whole range of activities. This can be an even more beneficial learning experience if you ensure that there are opportunities for evaluation, development and review of the process.

Finally, if you are managing or contributing to the team, you need to step back from doing the work to think about what the work is and how it should be managed, be it through peer observation, team teaching or the embedding of learning and teaching work into management activities. We learn from doing and from reflection on that action. In order to develop your own voice in learning and teaching you must strive to become a reflective practitioner.

Case study 17   Writing online learning materials

In her new post as a learning development librarian in a college, Frances was keen to make an impact on the learning and teaching experience of students and academic colleagues. The college had recently started to move into online and virtual learning environments, and on appointment Frances had been told that she would be responsible for developing some online learning materials that could be used by students for both self-directed and tutor-supported learning in key skills.

The nature of these online learning materials was not exactly specified. As far as she understood, the rather vague information and learning technology strategy had set some goals for key skills online and Frances was also hoping to sneak some information literacy content in as well. Although she was quite comfortable writing and designing web pages, she had limited experience of the key skills curriculum, using online assessment tools and questionnaire design, and soon realized that she needed some input from a teacher or educational technologist to help her make sense of this aspect of the project. She also needed some support and help from the IT people but she had found the college IT manager, Derek, a rather difficult character to work with, especially since he rarely left his office and smelt of burnt toast most days.

Six weeks into her job Frances received an e-mail, asking her to meet some of the college senior managers to discuss the plans for the online learning resource. At the meeting it was agreed that Frances should co-ordinate a short-term project team with three other people to produce and test the materials and have the resource ready to launch in two months. As Frances feared, she would be working with Derek the IT manager, and would be joined by two other people: the key skills co-ordinator, Sandy, and Clive who was a resources assistant. Clive was very interested in educational technology and actually ran a war-gaming website and online magazine in his spare time, but he was a junior member of staff.

The first meeting was not entirely successful. None of the people in the group had met each other apart from walking to and from the staff car park and, apart from Frances, Sandy was the only person who spoke.

Questions

1. What would you suggest Frances should try to do?
2. What difficulties might face her in leading this project successfully?

Discussion

Frances thought about what she might do next. She had wondered about whether to reconfigure the team in some way, changing people around or adding another person to the group who might help it gel a bit better. On reflection, though, she felt that the group was probably large enough already and what they needed to do was to get started.

She decided to go and speak to each member of the team individually and find out a bit more about their backgrounds and what they could contribute. First of all she went to see Sandy. Sandy was an experienced and semi-retired teacher, but she was a little fearful of online learning and teaching. She had a huge amount of experience and knowledge of key skills and ways you could support learning. Frances was certain that Sandy would be able to make an excellent contribution, probably through advising on the content and assessment approaches, but Sandy might not be very keen to get involved in the more technical elements.

Clive was a real web enthusiast, who loved writing and setting up web pages and showed a great flair for developing online materials. He wasn't very interested in content, but he was keen on planning and development work.

Derek was exceptionally shy and lived on toast, which he made in his office (despite comments from the site manager about health and safety). He had control over all the college's IT infrastructure and also was in charge of access to software. Frances still couldn't understand him, and had a difficult time trying to get him to agree to the access to the virtual learning environment (VLE) that she needed for her work. After meeting Derek and exchanging some e-mails, Frances realized that he was actually trying his best to be helpful, but his shyness was putting up barriers. Virtual communication might be easier than face-to-face meetings.

It seemed then that she could turn this fragmented real team into a reasonable virtual project team. Frances and Sandy met together and reviewed the potential content. There was quite a lot of existing material that could be revised or developed into a web resource, and Sandy had a long list of online learning resources that could be linked to or reused in some way.

Frances and Clive then worked on converting the paper-based material into web pages. Frances realized that she was able to use her information professional's skills in organizing information to very good effect in planning the structure of the pages and Clive had lots of interesting little ideas and tips for arranging the content. In particular he was much better at manipulating graphics and turned the text-heavy print materials into much more pleasing visual representations and diagrams. The main problem was that it took him a long time to get this done, and Frances ended up buying in his time to work on the project using her tiny resource development budget.

Derek was not involved to any great extent until the closing days of the project, which took longer to complete than initially planned, although everything was ready to go live in five months. Before the launch date, Frances realized that they needed to do an evaluation so she asked Sandy to work through the materials. Sandy's response to the resource was fairly neutral and Frances didn't know whether it was because she was too familiar with the content, disliked the online format or thought the whole thing didn't work. Frances then asked Sandy to find some students who could help with the evaluation. The student feedback from the evaluation was positive, and they made a few constructive suggestions, which Frances was able to action very quickly.

When the launch day arrived, Frances was delighted to see that the resource was working even better than planned. Derek had set up links to it from lots of different parts of the college intranet as well as the VLE and added some clever tracking and updating bits without being asked.

After the project ended Clive moved jobs within the college, becoming more directly involved with e-learning support and development. Sandy carried on doing much the same kind of work as before, but Frances noticed that she was more likely to refer students to the library and learning resources than she had previously. Derek seemed unchanged.

Frances reflected on what she had learnt from the project. She had liked working with this fairly disparate bunch and had learned different things from each of them. Sandy had provided the input of an experienced teacher. Clive had needed some proactive management, but had responded very well to collaboration, and had even gained some accidental career benefit. Derek was willing but needed to be handled on his own terms. For her part Frances had got insight into the academic life of the college from Sandy, practical experience in her work with Clive and had built up a shy rapport with Derek.

The next challenge was to develop the resource so it could be used outside the college. A lifelong learning partnership had been established involving the local public and university libraries as well as Frances' college, and one of the college's main inputs to the partnership would be access to and development of these learning support materials.

This would be, Frances suspected, a completely different kind of collaborative experience, but she was looking forward to the challenge.

Case study 18   Classroom and peer observation in practice

In the university where David (a team leader), Andrew and Pat (both subject librarians) worked, classroom observation was standard practice in the academic departments. Lecturers were observed by more senior academics and the reports of the observation were fed into the appraisal process. Because observation was linked to appraisal the assessment reports were kept confidential, and were used only as the trigger to academic appraisal. Some of the staff in the information services department were supposed to join in this process because they were on academic contracts, but as a practice it was not actively followed.

In fact, there seemed to be a mixed economy in terms of the development and review of learning and teaching activities within information services. Staff seemed quite happy to collaborate and share in induction activities, but they were deeply protective of the more advanced work they did in their subject areas. It was very hard to build consensus about the direction of their work in learning support, and in practice teaching was seen as an individual activity separate from much of the other team-based work within the department.

The status quo changed when an assistant director responsible for planning, administration and staff development was appointed. She was insistent that classroom observation be adopted, even if it were not required for the appraisal system used in the department. All the team leaders, including David, were trained in classroom observation practice and procedures and the scheme was introduced at the beginning of the academic year.

Observations took place though sometimes in a fairly haphazard way. Observers were occasionally given very short notice – 30 minutes was not unknown – and the observations were conducted in a mechanistic way, with an emphasis on correctly completing the paperwork, rather than learning from the process.

At the end of the year the management objective of introducing classroom observation had been met, but there had been no noticeable development in learning support practice.

Question

1. What recommendations would you make for changing the process?

Discussion

One option for David, Andrew and Pat was to carry on as before without changing. The formal mechanism was working within accepted levels so change was not compulsory, but our subject librarians and team leader were not entirely comfortable with the process.

All three of them had faced the first round of classroom observation with some anxiety. They were aware that the information from the process would feed into their appraisal and form part of their personnel record. This element meant that they were reluctant to share the results of the observation with each other, largely because of a fear of being seen to be weaker than each other. In its existing format classroom observation was not working as a development tool, either for individuals or for the department.

David, Andrew and Pat decided to experiment with peer observation and to try to build in opportunities to share best practice and to arrange collaborative development activities. This activity was going to run in parallel with formal classroom observation, and David would provide an evaluation after the end of the first year.

Arrangements were made for all people involved in observation to have training as observers as well as the observed. Someone from the central staff development unit ran a customized training session for all participants, and there were very clear messages about peer observation being kept separate from line management responsibilities and the opportunities for information-sharing and collaborative development.

After the training David, Andrew, Pat and their colleagues met briefly to discuss a schedule and plan for the peer observation programme. It was agreed that every member of the teaching team would observe one other person. They modified the standard university form, putting less emphasis on quantitative scores for the teaching, and creating more space for write-in commentary and space for descriptions of best practice and adding a few department-specific glosses (including comments on the use of ICT). It was agreed that the observations would take place over the course of the academic year, but that the process was still compulsory.

Arranging for the observation was now much easier than it had been since, rather than a few team leaders doing all the observations, everyone took part. Shyer staff were able to approach people they thought would be sympathetic, although there was some inevitable horse-trading about who would observe whom.

At the end of the teaching year in June a meeting for all the staff involved in the peer observation process took place. There were two main topics for discussion. In the first place, there was a short review of the process. Secondly, time was given over to people sharing best practice from their teaching sessions.

Most people felt more comfortable with the change from classroom to peer observation. Observation was seen to have shifted in focus from a judgement to a developmental activity, even if the reports still fed into appraisal. There was also a change in the way that the team members were reviewing their practice. Rather than focusing on their own work, many people had gained insight into other learning and teaching activities through being observers. From David's perspective, it seemed as if many of his colleagues had started to think more reflectively not just about their own work, but of the work of the whole department.

The sharing of best practice worked well. Even though staff were working with very different subject areas, there were a lot of examples of good practice in session design, delivery or assessment that other people could share and adapt. And people felt quite happy to open up and talk about what they were doing because they just needed to explain something they did well, and why.

In retrospect, David reflected, the shift from classroom to peer observation had had a more significant effect than the introduction of classroom observation. Peer observation was a much more inclusive process and it had been a very good team-building activity. Peer observation had been an initiative from within the teaching team, and it had helped to create a common identity and even a sense of purpose and direction. The staff had taken a more strategic and considered approach to their learning and teaching activities, moving away from concentrating on delivery to thinking about quality enhancement and collaboration.

The next stage, David and his colleagues decided, was to approach Bruce, one of the university's teacher fellows to act as a consultant in some of their development work. Now they felt more confident in their own practice, they could work with anyone!

10 Conclusions and the future

In the introduction we stated that this book is not about information literacy but about teaching and learning for information professionals. We have now reached a natural finishing point after reviewing the learning and teaching process in the preceding chapters, but we are conscious that much has been left unsaid.

Review of the themes in this book

We have covered topics in each chapter only briefly, since it was our deliberate intention to produce a general and accessible text. Whole works have been written on topics that we have covered in a mere paragraph. Our purpose was to provide a clear introduction to the subject, and we strove for simplicity in our approach rather than being simplistic.

In particular we have tried to avoid being either too prescriptive or too descriptive. In order to be effective at teaching and facilitating learning in any context you need to find your own way of doing things. You must take responsibility for your self-development. You cannot become an excellent teacher just by entering into a classroom, real or virtual, and following a set of rules. You need to learn from theory, experience and from reflection. We have shared plenty of practical tips with you, but tips stop you from making mistakes: they are not recipes for success.

In fact we have steered away from any recipes. We have taken a relativistic standpoint: you do what circumstances require that you do.

The environments in which you work will mean that you must take different approaches to developing and supporting information skills and information literacy among your client groups. This is the case at the level of delivery and also when you are developing your strategies and policies.

As a profession we may have some underlying principles and aspirations of the knowledge, skills and competences we want our learners to attain when we engage with them. These principles are now often gathered together in definitions of information literacy, but across our range of organizations and circumstances we are obliged to articulate them in different ways. We might give what are in effect the same learning outcomes different names. Even within the same university and the same teaching team, with humanities students we reinforce the academic value of library research skills (since this is the language validated within the faculty) whereas with business students we focus on business research skills (and relate them to the workplace). Some of the sources are identical and the fundamental outcomes should be very similar: students are able to find, identify and use academic and other material to support their studies and through this become information literate. We disguise the purpose with different names, but the fundamental values remain.

In terms of delivery, remember that your choice of method should be an active one. Do not fall into the trap of doing something because it has always been done that way. Consider instead the needs of your learners and your own as a teacher. You can reach the same final learning destination in a number of ways and should be willing to explore some different pathways.

At all times you must try to keep what you do meaningful and relevant, and test those objectives through assessment, feedback and evaluation. Of course what we mean by meaningful and relevant will vary. Good teaching is not just a popularity contest. It needs to be aligned with our teaching and learning objectives at an immediate and at a strategic level. As a profession we must accept the importance of our role in teaching and facilitating learning, both within formal education, in the workplace and in supporting lifelong learning. Just by writing this book we cannot engineer a shift to the recognition of the importance of information skills and information literacy. This is your task: you must be advocates and beacons of best practice. The best way of getting information skills recognized is through excellence and a clear articulation of your vision and values.

And there is so much good practice to share! We had a wealth of case study information on which we could draw, even if the final studies have a fictional element. We hope that our examples will inspire you to experiment within your teaching and to share your practice with colleagues and the wider community, by presenting workshops, writing up articles or just talking to people. There are very many excellent practitioners, but often they are invisible to the wider professional community.

Learning: a wider vision

As we pointed out in a previous chapter, libraries and information services should be the gateways to knowledge exploration and learning, both in real and virtual worlds. Many of our transactions with customers are about learning in the widest sense. If we could all learn autonomously, there would be no need for schools, or an educational system. Learning may be part of human nature, but teachers are often required to enable it. We must be conscious that learning happens in many settings, formal and informal, real and virtual, and we are engaged in many of those settings. Without jettisoning the values and core knowledge that make us information professionals we must embrace an understanding of learning and pedagogy and seek to integrate it within our practice.

There is a potential conflict, which is highlighted earlier in the book, that our role as a teacher structuring learning opportunities is different from the role of the information professional to support and guide. We move between models of dependency and independence. Many years ago one of the authors set an assignment that required students to compile an annotated bibliography. Some students would haunt the enquiry desks, try to get different members of staff to help them with each element. The boundary between what was appropriate enquiry support and what was over-helpful was blurred.

You too will find that you need to negotiate between your role as a teacher and as a member of support service, particularly in the way that you exercise authority and control with your learners. We do not mean this in the sense of a 19th-century school teacher, but the more experience you gather of teaching and facilitating learning in many settings, the more you realize that it is not exactly the same as enquiry work with a client.

Learning and technology

We do not really know whether the Google factor and the commoditization of knowledge will sound the death knell for libraries and information services of all kinds. If Google can index almost everything and end-users can buy direct from the best provider regardless of location, what future for intermediaries? When we write of learning and technology, are we thinking about technology as a learning space or a delivery mechanism? Let us now consider those two definitions.

How popular is technology-provided learning space, in the form of online discussion or the virtual learning environments (really more teaching and resource delivery environments, but that is another argument)? At the moment it seems that many pure e-learning educational ventures are not meeting their targets for student numbers or return on investment, most notably the UK e-university (McLeod, 2004). With the exception of a small number of pioneering organizations, this form of e-learning (technology-mediated distance learning) has not proved as popular as we might have predicted two or three years ago. At the same time blended e-learning, mixing conventional face-to-face teaching with online environments, is becoming standard practice within educational institutions. Online learning is less-developed in the private sector, but has definite potential as a training tool − but remember that learning is not synonymous with training! In the UK, the government white paper *Towards a Unified E-Learning Strategy* (Great Britain, Department for Education and Skills, 2003), had a bold vision for e-learning (or e-teaching at least) as a force for social inclusion throughout the home nations.

The other form of interaction with technology in learning is in using electronic information resources and software programs. Perhaps in the

1990s in the UK, and maybe in some other countries, we conflated teaching with training people to use technology. As early adopters of the internet librarians perhaps assumed that it was entirely our domain, and were a little surprised when it became common territory. Even now information literacy is often regarded as being about the use of technology rather than the broader definition of information. Our second weakness is in centring our thinking around resources. Teaching is sometimes built around using a resource, a piece of software or systems, which should be intuitive to use but which are not. Instead we must always focus on the learner. Increasingly the location of a resource matters less than its content, especially when so much is web-based and portals are ever more common.

Your authors suspect that university students at least are returning to academic resources after the initial passionate embrace of the internet faded and waned. No longer novel, the internet is functional, a part of everyday life for the majority of the population in the developed world. Since the glamour has worn off, people see that content is what matters, and it must be fit for its purpose, and that is not always the case with the internet. This does not happen by magic, and in our universities at least it will happen by changing assessment so that more value is ascribed to effective use of information. As awareness with technology increases, we have an opportunity to move beyond IT and to focus on information fundamentals.

When we planned this book we thought that in our conclusion we would provide you with a vision for the future of teaching and facilitating learning, developing the scenarios we described in our introduction in Chapter 1. By the end of our exploration, we are less sure that they will actually change. We will still have different contexts for our teaching, ranging from content-led to support-led environments, and many variations in between. Sometimes we will be working online, at other times directly with learners.

Library and information professionals and our role in learning

There are three challenges: identity, collaboration and visibility.

Depending on how your role in learning and teaching evolves, you may find that you develop a dual professional identity, as an information professional and as a teacher. This does not mean abandoning your existing values, it is rather an extension and evolution into someone who can function effectively in both roles. As you gain experience you may find that you have two separate paths for professional and career development. On the one hand there is the world you already know of professional engagement with colleagues in the same occupational area. You will have a shared language and common concerns linked to information literacy and the teaching of information skills, as well as other library and information work. On the other hand, your teaching identity will be developed through collaboration with a different group of professionals. You may need to navigate between these two worlds, establishing your dual identity. There are many synergies between those roles, which will enable you to grow and develop in both parts of your professional life.

The next challenge is that of collaboration, within and across organizations, inside the library and information world and outside. The accessibility of library and information services means that we have great opportunities to support the knowledge economy and bridge the digital divide. We will need to engage across sectors and with competing organizations to meet our aspirations of information literate societies. Already there are examples of collaborative practice in Sunderland in the UK and in the US (Cox, 2003; Nutefall, 2001), but these must grow in significance. As academic librarians, one of the key learning points for us when producing this book was finding out about the outstanding work in teaching and learning happening in other sectors. We had, naïvely, assumed that university libraries were leading the way. What we found was that, although much more is written and reported about work in academic libraries, good practice is everywhere, and we need to learn from each other, in order to change and enhance practice for all.

Finally, there is the issue of visibility, both in your role as a teacher and for information literacy itself. Throughout the book we have argued that the starting point for visibility will be professional credibility, achieved through excellence in practice. On another level is recognition of our work and role in teaching and supporting learning. In the UK, at the same time that MLA published its guidelines *Inspiring Learning for All* (MLA, 2003; MLA, 2004) a Government white paper was produced on e-learning which made no mention of libraries and information services at all (Great Britain, Department for Education and Skills, 2003). We need to create an identity at a collective as well as an individual level, which is recognized by policy makers.

This identity should develop within our organizations and throughout the profession. We need to review and debate our practice and objectives within our sectors and with our stakeholders (following Bruce, Chesterton and Grimison, 2002, and McCartin and Feid, 2001). There are some areas for immediate action. Within schools there is a huge variation in information literacy practice ranging from the excellence described by Barrett and Danks (2003) to many instances where children do not develop any real awareness of the importance of finding, evaluating and referring to suitable material to support their study and research. We also need to recognize that information literacy is a life skill, not confined to further and higher education alone, but one that is required to function in the workplace and in everyday life as well as supporting our lifelong learning. Already the evidence-based learning movement has changed healthcare practice, and information professionals are playing a key role.

And then we must be aware within the library and information profession that our role is shifting, from encouraging dependency to supporting and guiding independence in the quest for information, knowledge and, ultimately, wisdom.

Bibliography

ACRL's Institute for Information Literacy (2003) Characteristics of Programs of Information Literacy that Illustrate Best Practice, *College & Research Libraries News* **64** (1), 32–5.

Allan, B. (2002) *E-learning and Teaching in Library and Information Services*, London, Facet Publishing.

American Library Association (2003) *Introduction to Information Literacy*, www.ala.org/ala/acrl/acrlissues/acrlinfolit/infolitoverview/introtoinfolit/introinfolit.htm#what.

Anderson, R. S. and Speck, B. W. (1998) 'Oh What a Difference a Team Makes': why team teaching makes a difference, *Teaching and Teacher Education*, **14** (7), 671–86.

Anderson, S. (2003) *INFORMS: the information skills project. Final evaluation report*, available from http://informs.hud.ac.uk/informs/files/Final%20Evaluation%20Report.pdf.

Andretta, S. (2004) Visual Literacy, *Library and Information Update*, **3** (4), 26–7.

Atherton, J. S. (2003) *How to Teach*, Bedford, De Montfort University, www.dmu.ac.uk/~jamesa/teaching/.

Atherton, J. S. (2003) *Learners and Learning*, Bedford, De Montfort University, www.dmu.ac.uk/~jamesa/learning/index.htm.

Bandura, A. (1977) *Social Learning Theory*, Englewood Cliffs, Prentice Hall.

Bandura, A. (1986) *Social Foundations of Thought and Action: a social cognitive theory*, Englewood Cliffs, Prentice Hall.

Barker, P. (1998) Interactivity as an Extrinsic Motivating Force in Learning. In Brown, S., Armstrong, S. and Thompson, G. (eds), *Motivating Students*, London, Kogan Page, 7–14.

Barrett, L. and Danks, M. (2003) Information Literacy: a crucial role for schools, *Library and Information Update*, **2** (5), 42–4.

Bastable, W. et al. (n.d.) Wolverhampton, Department of Learning Resources, www.leeds.ac.uk/bigblue/wolverhampton.htm.

Baume, D. and Baume, C. (1996) *Learning to Teach: assessing students' work*, Oxford, Oxford Centre for Staff Development.

Bawden, D. (2001) Information and Digital Literacies: a review of concepts, *Journal of Documentation*, **57** (2), 218–59.

BBC Education (n.d.) Betsie Technical Outline, www.bbc.co.uk/education/betsie/tech.html/.

Biggs, J. (2003) *Teaching for Quality Learning at University*, 2nd edn, Buckingham, SRHE and Open University Press.

Bligh, D. (1998) *What's the Use of Lectures?* Exeter, Intellect Press.

Bloom, B. (ed.) (1956) *Taxonomy of Educational Objectives: the classification of educational goals*, New York, Longmans.

Bobby (n.d.) Available at http://bobby.watchfire.com/bobby/html/en/index.jsp.

Booth, A. and Brice, A. (eds) (2004) *Evidence-based Practice for Information Professionals: a handbook*, London, Facet Publishing.

Boydell, T. and Leary, M. (1996) *Identifying Training Needs, Training Essentials*, London, Institute of Personnel and Development.

Bråten, I and Olaussen, B. (2000) Motivation in College: understanding Norwegian college students' performance on the LASSI motivation subscale and their beliefs about academic motivation, *Learning and Individual Differences*, **12**, 177–87.

Brown, S. and Knight, P. (1994) *Assessing Learners in Higher Education*, London, Kogan Page.

Brown, S., Armstrong, S. and Thompson, G. (eds) (1998) *Motivating Students*, London, Kogan Page.

Bruce, C. (1997) *The Seven Faces of Information Literacy*, Blackwood, Auslib Press.

Bruce, C., Chesterton, P. and Grimison, C. (2002) Constituting Collective Consciousness: information literacy in university curricula, *International Journal for Academic Development*, **7** (1), 31–40.

Buchanan, D. (2000) An Eager and Enduring Embrace: the ongoing rediscovery of teamworking as a management idea. In Procter, S. and Mueller, F. (eds), *Teamworking*, Basingstoke, Palgrave Macmillan, 25–42.

Buchanan, D. and Huczynski, A. (2004) *Organizational Behaviour: an introductory text*, 5th edn, London, Financial Times Prentice Hall.

Buckley, F. J. (2000) *Team Teaching: what, why, and how?* Thousand Oaks, Sage.

Busato, V. et al. (1999) The Relation between Learning Styles, the Big Five Personality Traits and Achievement Motivation in Higher Education, *Personality and Individual Differences*, **26**, 129–40.

Clutterbuck, D. (2001) *Everyone Needs a Mentor: fostering talent at work*, London, Chartered Institute of Personnel and Development.

Core, J. (1999) EduLib: the programme closes but lives on, *Relay*, **48**, 14.

Corrall, S. (2003) *Information Capability: the need for professional leadership*, London, CILIP.

Cottrell, S. (2001) *Teaching Study Skills and Supporting Learning*, Basingstoke, Palgrave.

Cox, F. (2003) The Digital Divide: opportunities for information literacy, *Technology and Teacher Education Annual*, **2**, 875–8.

Critical Appraisal Skills Programme (2004) *CASP Appraisal Tools*, www.phru.nhs.uk/casp/appraisa.htm.

Curry, L. (1983) An Organization of Learning Styles Theory and Constructs, ERIC Document 235, 185.

Curry, L. (1990) A Critique of the Research on Learning Styles, *Educational Leadership*, **48**, 50–6.

D'Andrea, V. (1996) *Course Design Workshop Materials*, London, Roehampton Institute.

D'Andrea, V. (1999) Organizing Teaching and Learning: outcomes-based assessment. In Fry, H., Ketteridge, S. and Marshall, S. (eds), *A Handbook for Teaching and Learning in Higher Education: enhancing academic practice*, London, Kogan Page, 41–57.

Donnelly, A and Craddock, C. (2002) Information Literacy at Unilever R&D, *Library and Information Update*, **1** (9), 40–2.

Duarte, D. L. and Snyder, N. (2001) *Mastering Virtual Teams: strategies, tools, and techniques that succeed*, 2nd edn, San Francisco, Jossey Bass.

Eisenberg, M. B. and Berkowitz, R. E. (1990) *Information Problem Solving: the Big Six Skills approach to library and information skills instruction*, Norwood, New Jersey, Ablex Publishing.

Fox, D. (n.d.) *Team Teaching in Higher Education*, SCED paper 11, Birmingham, Standing Conference on Educational Development.

Franken, R. E. (1998) *Human Motivation*, 4th edn, Pacific Grove, Brooks/Cole.

Fry, H., Ketteridge, S. and Marshall, S. (eds) (1999) *A Handbook for Teaching and Learning in Higher Education: enhancing academic practice*, London, Kogan Page.

Gardner, H. (1983) *Frames of Mind*, New York, Basic Books.

Gardner, H. (2003) *Multiple Intelligences after Twenty Years*, Paper at American Educational Research Association, Chicago, Illinois, 21 April.

Gibbs, G. and Habeshaw, T. (1989) *Preparing to Teach*, Bristol, Technical and Educational Services.

Gibbs, G. and Haigh, M. (1984) *Designing Course Evaluation Questionnaires*, Oxford, Oxford Polytechnic.

Godwin, P. (2003) 'Information Literacy, But at What Level? In Martin, A. and Rader, H. (eds), *Information and IT Literacy: enabling learning in the 21st century*, London, Facet Publishing, 88–98.

Great Britain, Department for Education and Skills (2003) *Towards a Unified E-learning Strategy: consultation document*, Nottingham, Department for Education and Skills.

Great Britain, Quality Assurance Agency for Higher Education. (2004) *Benchmarking Academic Standards*, www.qaa.ac.uk/crntwork/benchmark/index.htm.

Herzberg, F. (1968) *Work and the Nature of Man*, London, Staples Press.

Hofstede, G. (2001) *Culture's Consequences: comparing values, behaviors, institutions and organizations across nations*, 2nd edn, Thousand Oaks, Sage.

Honey, P. and Mumford, A. (1992) *The Manual of Learning Styles*, 3rd edn, Maidenhead, Peter Honey.

Hounsell, D., Tait, H. and Day, K. (1997) *Feedback on Courses and Programmes of Study*, Edinburgh, Centre for Teaching, Learning and Assessment.

The Information Literacy Place, http://dis.shef.ac.uk/literacy/default.htm/.

Informs: The Information Skills Project, http://informs.hud.ac.uk/.

Isroff, K. and del Soldato, T. (1998) Students' Motivation in Higher Education Contexts. In Brown, S., Armstrong, S. and Thompson, G. (eds), *Motivating Students*, London, Kogan Page, 73–82.

Järvelä, S. and Niemivirta, M. (1999) The Changes in Learning Theory and the Topicality of Recent Research on Motivation, *Research Dialogue in Learning and Instruction*, **1**, 57–65.

Jarvis, P., Holford, J. and Griffin, C. (1998) *The Theory and Practice of Learning*, London, Kogan Page.

Johnston, B. and Webber, S. (2003) Information Literacy in Higher Education: a review and case study, *Studies in Higher Education*, **28** (3), 335–52.

Julien, H. and Given, L., (2003) Faculty–Librarian Relationships in the Information Literacy Context: a content analysis of librarians' expressed attitudes and experiences, *Canadian Journal of Information and Library Science*, **27** (3), 65–87.

Kolb, D. (1984) *Experiential Learning*, Englewood Cliffs, Prentice Hall.

Laurillard, D. (2002) *Rethinking University Teaching: a conversational framework for the effective use of learning technologies*, 2nd edn, London, Routledge.

Learning and Teaching Support Network Generic Centre. www.ltsn.ac.uk/.

LibLearn, www.ncl.ac.uk/library/liblearn.html.

Light, G. and Cox, R. (2001) *Learning and Teaching in Higher Education*, London, Paul Chapman.

Maslow, A. H. (1954) *Motivation and Personality*, New York, Harper.

McCartin, M. and Feid, P. (2001) Information Literacy for Undergraduates: where have we been and where are we going? *Advances in Librarianship*, **25**, 1– 27.

McLeod, D. (2004) The Online Revolution: mark II, *Guardian,* Higher Education, 13 April, 18–19.

McNamara, D. and Core, J. (1998) *Teaching for Learning in Libraries and Information Services: a series of educational workshops*, The EduLib Project and its teaching materials, Hull, EduLib Project.

McNicol, S. (2002) Learning in Libraries: lessons for staff, *New Library World*, **103** (7/8), 251–8.

Mead, G. H. (1950) *Mind, Self and Society from the Standpoint of a Behaviourist*, Chicago, University of Chicago Press.

Michel, S. (2001) What Do They Really Think? Assessing student and faculty perspectives of a web-based tutorial to library research, *College & Research Libraries*, **62** (4), 317–32

Micholls, J. G. (1984) Achievement Motivation: conceptions of the nature of ability, subjective experience, task choice and performance, *Psychological Review*, **91**, 328–46.

Milne, D. and Noone, S. (1996) *Teaching and Training for Non-teachers*, Leicester, BPS Books.

Mullins, L. (2002) *Management and Organisational Behaviour*, Harlow, Financial Times Prentice Hall.

Museums, Libraries and Archives Council (2003) *Inspiring Learning for All*, www.mla.gov.uk/documents/insplearn_il4a200005.doc.

Museums, Libraries and Archives Council (2004) *Inspiring Learning For All: a vision for accessible learning in museums, libraries and archives*, London, MLA, www.mla.gov.uk/action/learnacc/00insplearn.asp.

National Committee of Inquiry into Higher Education (1997) *Higher Education in the Learning Society*, London, HMSO [Dearing Report].

New London Group (1996) A Pedagogy of Multiliteracies: designing social futures, *Harvard Educational Review*, **66**, 60–92.

Nichols, J. (ed.) (1984) *The Development of Achievement Motivation*, London, JAI Press.

Nutefall, J. (2001) Information Literacy: developing partnerships across library types, *Research Strategies*, **18**, 311–18

Parlett, M. and Hamilton, D. (1977) Evaluation as Illumination. In Parlett, M. and Deardon, G. (eds), *Introduction to Illuminative Evaluation: studies in higher education*. Cardiff-by-Sea CA, Pacific Soundings Press. Cited in Light, G. and Cox, R. (2001) *Learning and Teaching in Higher Education*, London, Paul Chapman.

Pask, G. (1976) Styles and Strategies of Learning, *British Journal of Educational Psychology*, **46**, 128–48.

Peterson, R. (1992) *Managing Successful Learning: a practical guide for teachers and trainers*, London, Kogan Page.

Piaget, J. (1950) *The Psychology of Intelligence*, London, Routledge & Kegan Paul.

Powis, C. (2002) *Developing the Teaching Team: a workshop report from the CoFHE/UC&R Joint Conference*, April, unpublished. Available from jwebb@dmu.ac.uk or chris.powis@northampton.ac.uk.

Powis, C. (2004) Developing the Academic Librarian as Learning Facilitator. In Oldroyd, M. (ed.), *Developing Academic Library Staff for Future Success*, London, Facet Publishing.

Race, P. (ed.) (1999) *2000 Tips for Lecturers*, London, Kogan Page.

Race, P. and Brown, S. (1998) *The Lecturer's Toolkit*, London, Kogan Page.

Race, P. and Brown, S. (2001) *The ILTA Guide: inspiring learning about teaching and assessment*, York, Institute for Learning and Teaching in Higher Education in association with EducationGuardian.co.uk.

Ramsden, P. (1992) *Learning to Teach in Higher Education*, London, Routledge.

Rayner, S. and Riding, R. (1997) Towards a Categorisation of Cognitive Styles and Learning Styles, *Educational Psychology*, **17**, 5–28.

Salmon, G. (2000) *E-moderating*, London, Kogan Page.

Schon, D. A. (1982) *The Reflective Practitioner: how professionals think in action*, New York, Basic Books.

Schunk, D. H. (1981) Modelling and Attributional Feedback Effects on Children's Achievement: a self-efficacy analysis, *Journal of Educational Psychology*, **74**, 93–105.

SCONUL Advisory Committee on Information Literacy (1999) *Information Skills in Higher Education*, Briefing paper, London, SCONUL.

Seamans, N. (2002) Student Perceptions of Information Literacy: insights for librarians, *Reference Services Review*, **30** (2), 112–23.

Sippings, G. (2004) Putting Information on the Map at the Inland Revenue, *Library and Information Update*, **3** (4), 30–3.

Skinner, B. F. (1954) The Science of Learning and the Art of Teaching, *Harvard Educational Review*, **24**, 88–97.

Squires, G. (1994) *A New Model of Teaching and Training*, Hull, University of Hull.

Stipek, D. (2002) Good Instruction is Motivating. In Wigfield, A. and Eccles, J. S. *Development of Achievement Motivation*, San Diego, Academic Press, 309–32.

VARK: a guide to learning styles, www.vark-learn.com/english/index.asp.

Vidmar, D. (1998) Affective Change: integrating pre-sessions in the students' classroom prior to library instruction, *Reference Services Review* (Fall/Winter), 75–95 .

Vygotsky, L. (1978) *Mind in Society: the development of higher psychological processes*, London, Harvard University Press

Williamson, M. (1993) *Training Needs Analysis*, Library Training Guides, London, Library Association Publishing.

Zimmerman, B. (2000) Self-efficacy: an essential motive to learn, *Contemporary Education Psychology*, **25**, 82–91.

Index

Information and IT Literacy
Enabling learning in the 21st century

Edited by Allan Martin and Hannelore Rader

'I found the structure well conceived, the main issues largely explored, and the contents eminently readable overall.'　　　　　　　　　　　　　　　　　FREEPINT

As our global society becomes increasingly dependent on accessing and using information, the preparation of individuals to be effective information users - as learners, as employees and as citizens - is becoming an imperative. Until recently it has been common to view IT literacy and information literacy from two different perspectives, but these are now converging in educational contexts as integrated IT-supported and managed learning environments become the norm.

This groundbreaking book contains a collection of selected and invited papers from foremost practitioners in the field and is edited in consultation with an international editorial board. It surveys and analyses current practice, emerging directions and ongoing issues relating to information and IT literacy, focusing on all aspects of learning enablement, including education and training worldwide, lifelong learning and e-learning. The contributions confirm a diversity of activity and the emergence of a new community of practice, the e-literacy community.

The book is organized into four parts: Part 1: Contexts; Part 2: Exploring the Seven Pillars model; Part 3: Challenges to Implementation; and Part 4: Research Perspectives. Topics covered include:

- defining e-literacy
- models of e-literacy
- global perspectives
- strategies for implementation
- assessment
- certification and accreditation
- cost-effectiveness of programmes
- programme and course structures
- integrating e-literacy into educational practice
- auditing provision
- examining users' perspectives.

This book is essential reading for all information and education practitioners needing to develop and manage integrated learning environments, including librarians, IT personnel, student support staff, lifelong learning providers, and government and other agencies. It will also be of great interest to students and researchers in the field.

2003; 304pp; hardback; 1-85604-463-7; £39.95

Developing Academic Library Staff for Future Success

EDITED BY MARGARET OLDROYD

In a climate of rapid change – growth in student numbers, new e-learning methods, the need to manage resources on a value-for-money basis, and the move towards the digital library – staff development is a key area of concern for university and college library managers. Success in the development of all staff, as part of a coherent approach to human resource management, is critical in delivering the strategic and operational objectives of any forward-looking library service.

This book looks at the place of staff development in the current and future strategic management of academic libraries. It highlights how roles are changing and evaluates the implications of this for skill needs and development routes. The contributors are practising managers in education institutions, and their contributions are illustrated by drawing on their own experience, using material from case studies and relevant international initiatives. Contributions include:

- human resources for higher education in the 21st century
- rethinking professional competence for the networked environment
- developing the academic library managers of the future
- converging on staff development
- developing the academic librarian as learning facilitator
- development routes for academic library support staff
- lifelong learning at work: staff development for the flexible workforce
- delivering staff development using a virtual learning environment
- collaborative staff development
- taking the strategic approach to staff development.

This book is essential reading for all current and future academic library managers as well as institutional managers and staff developers.

The contributors
Moira Bent , Sheila Corrall, Philippa Dolphin, Biddy Fisher, Sally Neocosmos, Patrick Noon, Margaret Oldroyd, Chris Powis, Margaret Weaver, Jo Webb, Sue White.

2004; 208pp; hardback; 1-85604-478-5; £39.95

E-Learning and Teaching in Library and Information Services

Barbara Allan

Networked technologies are dramatically changing education and training, as they enable people to access more and more information online and to communicate with others across boundaries of place and time. Online learning is an increasingly important approach to user education, information literacy and LIS staff development. LIS professionals are becoming ever more involved in the business of e-learning and teaching, from designing and developing materials and programmes to supporting individual and group learning using virtual learning environments.

This stimulating new book provides an overview and guide to the rapidly developing field of virtual learning, and provides much-needed practical guidance in the development, use and delivery of online learning and teaching materials and programmes. It is presented in a readable and visually attractive style, with a wealth of examples, checklists, charts and tables. It also includes a wide range of case studies taken from the library and information world in the UK and worldwide.

The book is divided into three parts. The first provides an overview of current e-learning tools and technologies; the second offers guidance on e-learning and teaching skills and techniques; and the third considers the implications for the library and information profession. Key areas covered include:

- virtual communication tools
- integrated learning environments
- web-based training materials
- learning and teaching
- e-tutoring
- successful e-learning
- design of e-learning programmes and materials
- e-learning activities
- implications for the LIS profession
- resources.

This book is essential reading for anyone interested in online learning and teaching ideas, particularly LIS professionals involved in online learning and training, as well as students on library and information courses. It will also be of interest to staff development or personnel officers, trainers, consultants and other change agents, and is of international relevance.

2002; 288pp; hardback; 1-85604-439-4; £39.95